The Politics of Aesthetics

Also available from Continuum:

The Politics of Aesthetics

The Distribution of the Sensible

JACQUES RANCIÈRE

Translated with an Introduction by Gabriel Rockhill

continuum

Continuum International Publishing Group

The Tower Building, 11 York Road, London SE1 7NX
80 Maiden Lane, Suite 704, New York NY 10038

First published in France under the title *Le Partage du sensible: Esthétique et politique*
© La Fabrique-Éditions, 2000
© Gabriel Rockhill, 2004

First published 2004
Reprinted 2005
Paperback edition first published 2006
Reprinted 2006, 2007 (twice), 2008, 2011 (twice), 2012

British Library Cataloguing-in-Publication Data
A catalogue record for this book is available from the British Library.

ISBN 13: HB: 978-0-8264-7067-6
PB: 978-0-8264-8954-8

Typeset by Fakenham Photosetting, Norfolk
Printed and bound in the United States of America

Contents

Translator's Preface

The Reconfiguration of Meaning

GABRIEL ROCKHILL

Translation is often deplored, with a sense of self-satisfied disillusionment, as an impossible project. Since there are no objective criteria for evaluating the relationship between the source language and the target language, it is claimed that the latter remains fundamentally undetermined by the former. This situation has given birth to a myriad of possible responses: the cynical condemnation of all translation, the enthusiastic acceptance of the archipelago of independent language games, the valorization of translation as a unique form of writing with its own properly literary forms, the celebration of the abyss separating languages as an aesthetico-ethical opportunity to introduce a Proustian *langue étrangère dans la langue...*

These various reactions are at least correct in one respect: they reject the purportedly universal criteria of translation argued for by their adversaries (the deep structure of all discourse or the pure language whose echo can be heard in the interstices between individual languages). Nonetheless, this very polarization between universal translatability and the utter impossibility of a faithful rendering of the original – not to mention the middle ground cunningly occupied by those who declare translation to be at once possible and impossible – is in fact dependent on concrete criteria that provide an overall framework for thinking about translation.

The first of these criteria is, broadly speaking, historical. The conceptual network defining the basic elements and modalities of what is generally understood as translation is necessarily dependent on a historical situation. The very distinction between translation and adaptation, for example, has by no means remained a historical constant, and the same could be said of the relationship between original prose and plagiarism, transcription and revision, fidelity and infidelity.[1] In fact, these categories can only operate within a general logic of signification that confers meaning on them by situating them in a relational network. This explains why they are not even necessarily distributed according to the oppositions they appear to fall within and do not simply exist as empty categories whose content is provided by each new epoch. To put this point rather succinctly, the very meaning of 'translation' – and all of its corresponding parts – cannot be separated from the historical situation within which it functions.

The second major criterion is social. In order for a translation to be recognized as such and considered worthy of the name, it has to abide by the broad parameters operative in a particular community. These parameters need not necessarily impose a single model or method of translation, but they define the general coordinates within which translation can be distinguished from other discursive procedures. Each community establishes a logic of signification that presupposes a specific understanding of what meaning is, how it operates, the normative principles it should abide by, its function in social discourse, etc. Communities do, of course, come into conflict – both with themselves and with other communities –, but the basic point remains unchanged: just as the translator never works in a historical vacuum, translation is never an isolated soliloquy uninformed by a community. In short, translation is neither based on universal criteria nor is it condemned to a solitary encounter with the intractable original. It is a historical practice that always takes place – implicitly or explicitly – within a social framework.

This means that translation, as I propose to understand it under the current circumstances, is not simply a form of mediation between two distinct languages. It is a relational reconfiguration of meaning via a logic of signification that is rendered possible by a socio-historical situation. This process can, in fact, take place within a single language, which does not however mean that understanding itself is an act of translation or that we are condemned to endlessly paraphrasing our original ideas. An alternate logic of signification can actually use the exact same words to mean something entirely different because it determines the very structure of meaning, the horizons of what is qualified as language, the *modi operandi* of words and sentences, the entire network that defines the process of signification. Thus, when translation does occur between two languages, the overall logic of signification is often more important than the differences between the languages themselves because it determines the very limits between these two languages, how meaning operates in each of them, the semantic relationships that need to be preserved and those that can be discarded, etc.

Prior to being a choice about certain words, the act of translation is a choice concerning the logic of signification in which these words function. In the case of the present translation, I have chosen to distance myself from one of the dominant methods of translation for rendering contemporary French intellectuals in English, which is historically the heir to a logic of signification based on the inviolable sacred status of the original text. This method has led to the use of every possible typographical and etymological artifice to prove – with indisputable success in some cases – that it is impossible to translate between different languages. The end result has often been a sacred jargon of authenticity that is cunningly appropriated by the high priests of the unknown in order to reconstruct the original syntax behind the translation and unveil the unsaid in the said. Thus, in spite of its obsessive preoccupation with the impossibility of grasping the original text, this method of translation is paradoxically based on establishing the greatest possible typographic proximity to the sacred original. In fact, the ultimate telos of this method can only be described in terms of an asymptote where the vertical axis would be the verbatim identity between the translation and the original work (whose ultimate consequences were deduced by Borges' Pierre Menard).[2]

Rather than aiming at asymptotically transcribing Jacques Rancière's work into an idiom for the initiated, the following translation was made within the coordinates of an entirely different logic of signification. The primary unit of translation was not taken to be the typography of an individual word or the uniformity of a particular concept, but the entire relational system of signification at work. Strictly speaking, there is no basic unit of translation since there are only relations within and between systems of signification. This has meant abandoning the supposed autarchy of the individual text and the mantra-like motto 'sola scriptura' in order to analyse the relational network within which Rancière's work has emerged. More specifically, it has required studying, in both French and English, Rancière's entire corpus, his standard historical references (from Plato and the New Testament to Balzac and Rossellini), and the work of his contemporary interlocutors. The objective of the current translation might therefore best be described in terms of a relational reconfiguration of meaning that recasts Rancière's work in an alternate system of signification. This reconfiguration inevitably masks certain aspects of his work in French, but hopefully only insofar as it simultaneously opens up the possibility that other aspects thereby become visible.

Only part of the current publication is a translation of Jacques Rancière's *Le Partage du sensible: Esthétique et politique* (Paris: La Fabrique–éditions, 2000). In addition to a brief introduction to Rancière's work and an afterword by Slavoj Žižek, the reader will also find an interview conducted for the English edition, a glossary of technical terms, and a bibliography of primary and secondary sources.

I would like to extend a special thanks to Tristan Palmer, who originally agreed to take on this project, as well as to the current editorial staff at Continuum Books (Hywel Evans, Sarah Douglas, and John Cox) that has allowed me to see it through to completion. I would also like to personally acknowledge the invaluable contribution made by Radmila Djordjevic as well as by Emiliano Battista, Pierre-Antoine Chardel, Andrew Parker, Ludovic Soutif and Yves Winter. Finally, my gratitude to Jacques Rancière is inestimable. In addition to agreeing to an interview for the English edition, he has taken the time to clarify certain passages and has provided helpful suggestions concerning the glossary and bibliography. His generous contribution has helped make the current volume much more than a translation of the original French publication.

Translator's Introduction

Jacques Rancière's Politics of Perception[3]

GABRIEL ROCKHILL

As Alain Badiou has aptly pointed out, Jacques Rancière's work does not belong to any particular academic community but rather inhabits unknown intervals 'between history and philosophy, between philosophy and politics, and between documentary and fiction' (1998: 122). His unique methodology, eclectic research habits, and voracious propensity for assimilating European intellectual and cultural history are comparable perhaps only to the unclassifiable work of Michel Foucault, an author with whom he himself acknowledges certain affinities. If his voice has yet to be heard in full force in the English-speaking world due to a lack of translations and sufficient secondary literature, it is perhaps attributable to what Rancière himself has called the distribution of the sensible, or the system of divisions and boundaries that define, among other things, what is visible and audible within a particular aesthetico-political regime.

Although closely affiliated with the group of neo-Marxists working around Althusser in the 1960s, Rancière's virulent criticisms of the latter as of 1968 served to distance him from the author with whom he had shared the common project *Lire le Capital* in 1965. As Rancière explained in the Preface to *La Leçon d'Althusser* (1974), the theoretical and political distance separating his work from Althusserian Marxism was partially a result of the events of 1968 and the realization that Althusser's school was a 'philosophy of order' whose very principles anaesthetized the revolt against the bourgeoisie. Uninspired by the political options proposed by thinkers such as Deleuze and Lyotard, Rancière saw in the politics of difference the risk of reversing Marx's statement in the *Thesis on Feuerbach*: 'We tried to transform the world in diverse ways, now it is a matter of interpreting it' (1974: 14). These criticisms of the response by certain intellectuals to the events of May 1968 eventually led him to a critical re-examination of the social, political, and historical forces operative in the production of theory.

In the first two books to follow the collection of essays on Althusser, Rancière explored a question that would continue to preoccupy him in his later work: from what position do we speak and in the name of what or whom? Whereas *La Nuit des prolétaires* (1981) proceeded via the route of meticulous historical research to unmask the illusions of representation and give voice to certain mute events in the history of workers' emancipation, *Le Philosophe et ses pauvres* (1983) provided a conceptualization of the relationship between thought and society, philosophic representation and its concrete historical object. Both of these works contributed to undermining the privileged position usurped by philosophy in its various attempts to speak for others, be it the proletariat, the poor, or anyone else who is not 'destined to think'. However, far from advocating a populist stance and claiming to finally bestow a specific identity on the underprivileged, Rancière thwarted the artifice at work in the discourses founded on the singularity of the other by revealing the ways in which they are ultimately predicated on keeping the other in its place.

This general criticism of social and political philosophy was counter-balanced by a more positive account of the relationship between the 'intellectual' and the emancipation of society in Rancière's fourth book, *Le Maître ignorant* (1987). Analysing the life and work of Joseph Jacotet, Rancière argued in favour of a pedagogical methodology that would abolish any presupposed inequalities of intelligence such as the academic hierarchy of master and disciple. For Rancière, equality should not be thought of in terms of a goal to be attained by working through the lessons promulgated by prominent social and political thinkers. On the contrary, it is the very axiomatic point of departure whose sporadic reappearance via disturbances in the set system of social inequalities is the very essence of emancipation. This explains, in part, Rancière's general rejection of political philosophy, understood as the theoretical enterprise that abolishes politics proper by identifying it with the 'police' (see below). It also sheds light on his own attempt to work as an 'ignorant schoolmaster' who – rather than transmitting performatively contradictory lessons on the content of emancipation – aims at giving a voice to those excluded from the hierarchies of knowledge.

With the more recent publication of *Aux Bords du politique* (1990) and *La Mésentente* (1995), Rancière has further elaborated a politics of democratic emancipation, which might best be understood in terms of its central concepts. The *police*, to begin with, is defined as an organizational system of coordinates that establishes a distribution of the sensible or a law that divides the community into groups, social positions, and functions. This law implicitly separates those who take part from those who are excluded, and it therefore presupposes a prior aesthetic division between the visible and the invisible, the audible and the inaudible, the sayable and the unsayable. The essence of *politics* consists in interrupting the distribution of the sensible by supplementing it with those who have no part in the perceptual coordinates of the community, thereby modifying the very aesthetico-political field of possibility. It is partially for this reason that Rancière defines *the political* as relational in nature, founded on the intervention of politics in the police order rather than on the establishment of a particular governmental regime. Moreover, politics in its strict sense never presupposes a reified subject or predefined group of individuals such as the proletariat, the poor, or minorities. On the contrary, the only possible subject of politics is the *people* or the *dēmos*, i.e. the supplementary part of every account of the population. Those who have no name, who remain invisible and inaudible, can only penetrate the police order via a mode of *subjectivization* that transforms the aesthetic coordinates of the community by implementing the universal presupposition of politics: we are all equal. *Democracy* itself is defined by these intermittent acts of political subjectivization that reconfigure the communal distribution of the sensible. However, just as *equality* is not a goal to be attained but a presupposition in need of constant verification, democracy is neither a form of government nor a style of social life. Democratic *emancipation* is a random process that redistributes the system of sensible coordinates without being able to guarantee the absolute elimination of the social inequalities inherent in the police order.

The irresolvable conflict between politics and the police, most visible perhaps in the perennial persistence of a *wrong* that cannot be resolved by juridical litigation, has led many readers to interpret *La Mésentente* as a simple continuation of Lyotard's *Le Différend* (1983). Although a conceptual proximity is readily apparent, Rancière is careful to distinguish his project from what he considers to be the essentially discursive nature of *le différend*. According to his definition, *disagreement* is neither a misunderstanding nor a general lack of comprehension. It is a conflict over what is meant by 'to speak' and over the very distribution of the sensible that delimits the horizons of the sayable and determines the relationship between seeing, hearing, doing, making, and thinking. In other words, disagreement is less a clash between heterogeneous phrase regimens or genres of discourse than a conflict between a given distribution of the sensible and what remains outside it.

Beginning with the publication of *Courts Voyages au pays du peuple* (1990) and up to his most recent work on film and modern art, Rancière has repeatedly foregrounded his long-standing interest in aesthetics while at the same time analysing its conjunction with both politics and history. In positioning himself against the Sartrean preoccupation with *engagement* and the more recent hegemony of the *Tel Quel* group, Rancière presents his reader with a unique account of aesthetics as well as an innovative description of its major regimes. According to the genealogy he has undertaken, the *ethical regime* of images characteristic of Platonism is primarily concerned with the origin and telos of imagery in relationship to the ethos of the community. It establishes a distribution of images – without, however, identifying 'art' in the singular – that rigorously distinguishes between artistic simulacra and the 'true arts' used to educate the citizenry concerning their role in the communal body. The *representative regime* is an artistic system of Aristotelian heritage that liberates imitation from the constraints of ethical utility and isolates a normatively autonomous domain with its own rules for fabrication and criteria of evaluation. The *aesthetic regime* of art puts this entire system of norms into question by abolishing the dichotomous structure of *mimēsis* in the name of a contradictory identification between *logos* and pathos. It thereby provokes a transformation in the distribution of the sensible established by the representative regime, which leads from the primacy of fiction to the primacy of language, from the hierarchical organization of genres to the equality of represented subjects, from the principle of appropriate discourse to the indifference of style with regard to subject matter, and from the ideal of speech as act and performance to the model of writing.

Rancière has forcefully argued that the emergence of literature in the nineteenth century as distinct from *les belles-lettres* was a central catalyst in the development of the aesthetic regime of art. By rejecting the representative regime's poetics of *mimēsis*, modern literature contributed to a general reconfiguration of the sensible order linked to the contradiction inherent in what Rancière calls *literarity*, i.e. the status of a written word that freely circulates outside any system of legitimation. On the one hand, literarity is a necessary condition for the appearance of modern literature as such and its emancipation from the representative regime of art. However, it simultaneously acts as the contradictory limit at which the specificity of literature itself disappears due to the fact that it no longer has any clearly identifiable characteristics that would distinguish it from any other mode of discourse. This partially explains the other major form of writing that has been in constant struggle with democratic literarity throughout the modern age: the idea of a 'true writing' that would incorporate language in such a way as to exclude the free-floating, disembodied discourse of literarity. The 'positive contradiction' between these two forms of writing, as well as the paradox that defines the unique discursive status of literature as such, has given rise to numerous and varied responses through the course of time. In other words, this contradiction has played a productive role in the emergence of modern literature, and it has also been decisive in setting the stage for later developments in the aesthetic regime of art. To take one example among many, Rancière has recently argued in *La Fable cinéma-tographique* (2001) that a positive contradiction – between elements of the representative and aesthetic regimes of art – is also operative in film. On the one hand, the very invention of film materially realized the properly aesthetic definition of art, first elaborated in Schelling's *System of Transcendental Idealism*, as a union of conscious and unconscious processes. On the other hand, however, film is an art of fiction that bestows a new youth on the genres, codes, and conventions of representation that democratic literarity had put into question.

In his critical genealogy of art and politics, Rancière has also dealt extensively with the emergence of history as a unique discipline (*Les*

Noms de l'histoire, 1992) and, more recently, with psychoanalysis (*L'Inconscient esthétique*, 2000), photography, and contemporary art (*Le Destin des images*, 2003). Behind the intricate analyses present in each of these studies, a central argument is discernible: the historical conditions of possibility for the appearance of these practices are to be found in the contradictory relationship between elements of the representative and aesthetic regimes of art. Thus continuing to work in the intervals between politics, philosophy, aesthetics, and historiography, Jacques Rancière will undoubtedly leave his own indelible mark on one of his privileged objects of study: the distribution of the sensible.

The Distribution of the Sensible

Foreword

The following pages respond to a twofold solicitation. At their origin was a set of questions asked by two young philosophers, Muriel Combes and Bernard Aspe, for their journal, *Alice*, and more specifically for the section entitled 'The Factory of the Sensible'. This section is concerned with aesthetic acts as configurations of experience that create new modes of sense perception and induce novel forms of political subjectivity. It is within this framework that they interviewed me on the consequences of my analyses—in *Disagreement*—of the distribution of the sensible that is at stake in politics, and thus of a certain aesthetics of politics. Their questions, prompted as well by a novel reflection on the major avant-garde theories and experiments concerning the fusion of art and life, dictate the structure of the present text. At the request of Eric Hazan and Stéphanie Grégoire, I developed my responses and clarified their presuppositions [8] as far as possible.⁴

This particular solicitation is, however, inscribed in a broader context. The proliferation of voices denouncing the crisis of art or its fatal capture by discourse, the pervasiveness of the spectacle or the death of the image, suffice to indicate that a battle fought yesterday over the promises of emancipation and the illusions and disillusions of history continues today on aesthetic terrain. The trajectory of Situationist discourse – stemming from an avant-garde artistic movement in the post-war period, developing into a radical critique of politics in the 1960s, and absorbed today into the routine of the disenchanted discourse that acts as the 'critical' stand-in for the existing order – is undoubtedly symptomatic of the contemporary ebb and flow of aesthetics and politics, and of the transformations of avant-garde thinking into nostalgia. It is, however, the work of Jean-François Lyotard that best marks the way in which 'aesthetics' has become, in the last twenty years, the privileged site where the tradition of critical thinking has metamorphosed into deliberation on mourning. The reinterpretation of the Kantian analysis [9] of the sublime introduced into the field of art a concept that Kant had located beyond it. It did this in order to more effectively make art a witness to an encounter with the unpresentable that cripples all thought, and thereby a witness for the prosecution against the arrogance of the grand aesthetico-political endeavour to have 'thought' become 'world'. In this way, reflection on art became the site where a mise-en-scène of the original abyss of thought and the disaster of its misrecognition continued after the proclamation of the end of political utopias. A number of contemporary contributions to thinking the disasters of art or the image convert this fundamental reversal into more mediocre prose.

This familiar landscape of contemporary thought defines the context in which these questions and answers are inscribed, but it does not specify their objective. The following responses will not lay claim yet again, in the face of postmodern disenchantment, to the avant-garde vocation of art or to the vitality of a modernity that links the conquests of artistic innovation to the victories of emancipation. These pages do not have their origin in a desire to take a polemical stance. They are inscribed in a long-term project that aims at re-establishing a debate's conditions of intelligibility. This means, first of all, elaborating the very meaning of [10] what is designated by the term aesthetics, which denotes neither art theory in general nor a theory that would consign art to its effects on sensibility. Aesthetics refers to a specific regime for identifying and reflecting on the arts: a mode of articulation between ways of doing and making, their corresponding forms of visibility, and possible ways of thinking about their relationships (which presupposes a certain idea of thought's effectivity). Defining the connections within this aesthetic regime of the arts, the possibilities that they determine, and their modes of transformation, such is the present objective of my research and of a seminar held over the past few years within the framework provided by the University of Paris-VIII and the *Collège International de Philosophie*. The results of this research will not be found in the present work; their elaboration will follow its own proper pace. I have nevertheless attempted to indicate a few historical and conceptual reference points appropriate for reformulating certain problems that have been irremediably confused by notions that pass off conceptual prejudices as historical determinations and temporal delimitations as conceptual determinations. Among the foremost of these notions figures, of course, the concept of modernity, today the source of all the jumbled miscellany that arbitrarily sweeps [11] together such figures as Hölderlin, Cézanne, Mallarmé, Malevich, or Duchamp into a vast whirlwind where Cartesian science gets mixed up with revolutionary parricide, the age of the masses with Romantic irrationalism, the ban on representation with the techniques of mechanized reproduction, the Kantian sublime with the Freudian primal scene, the flight of the gods with the extermination of the Jews in Europe. Indicating the general lack of evidence supporting these notions obviously does not entail adhering to the contemporary discourses on the return to the simple reality of artistic practices and its criteria of assessment. The connection between these 'simple practices' and modes of discourse, forms of life, conceptions of thought, and figures of the community is not the fruit of a maleficent misappropriation. On the contrary, the effort to think through this connection requires forsaking the unsatisfactory mise-en-scène of the 'end' and the 'return' that persistently occupies the terrain of art, politics, and any other object of thought. [12]

The Distribution of the Sensible: Politics and Aesthetics

In Disagreement, *politics is examined from the perspective of what you call the 'distribution of the sensible'. In your opinion, does this expression provide the key to the necessary junction between aesthetic practices and political practices?*

I call the distribution of the sensible the system of self-evident facts of sense perception that simultaneously discloses the existence of something in common and the delimitations that define the respective parts and positions within it.[5] A distribution of the sensible therefore establishes at one and the same time something common that is shared and exclusive parts. This apportionment of parts and positions is based on a distribution of spaces, times, and forms of activity that determines the very manner in which something in common lends itself to participation and in what way various individuals have a part in this distribution. Aristotle states that a citizen is someone who *has a part* in the act of governing and being governed. However, another form of distribution precedes this act of partaking in government: the distribution that [13] determines those who have a part in the community of citizens. A speaking being, according to Aristotle, is a political being. If a slave understands the language of its rulers, however, he does not 'possess' it. Plato states that artisans cannot be put in charge of the shared or common elements of the community because they do *not have the time* to devote themselves to anything other than their work. They cannot be *somewhere else* because *work will not wait.* The distribution of the sensible reveals who can have a share in what is common to the community based on what they do and on the time and space in which this activity is performed. Having a particular 'occupation' thereby determines the ability or inability to take charge of what is common to the community; it defines what is visible or not in a common space, endowed with a common language, etc. There is thus an 'aesthetics' at the core of politics that has nothing to do with Benjamin's discussion of the 'aestheticization of politics' specific to the 'age of the masses'. This aesthetics should not be understood as the perverse commandeering of politics by a will to art, by a consideration of the people qua work of art. If the reader is fond of analogy, aesthetics can be understood in a Kantian sense – re-examined perhaps by Foucault – as the system of *a priori* forms determining what presents itself to sense experience. It is a delimitation of [14] spaces and times, of the visible and the invisible, of speech and noise, that simultaneously determines the place and the stakes of politics as a form of experience. Politics revolves around what is seen and what can be said about it, around who has the ability to see and the talent to speak, around the properties of spaces and the possibilities of time.

It is on the basis of this primary aesthetics that it is possible to raise the question of 'aesthetic practices' as I understand them, that is forms of visibility that disclose artistic practices, the place they occupy, what they 'do' or 'make' from the standpoint of what is common to the community. Artistic practices are 'ways of doing and making' that intervene in the general distribution of ways of doing and making as well as in the relationships they maintain to modes of being and forms of visibility. The Platonic proscription of the poets is based on the impossibility of doing two things at once prior to being based on the immoral content of fables. The question of fiction is first a question regarding the distribution of places. From the Platonic point of view, the stage, which is simultaneously a locus of public activity and the exhibition-space for 'fantasies', disturbs the clear partition of identities, activities, and spaces. The same is true of [15] writing. By stealing away to wander aimlessly without knowing who to speak to or who not to speak to, writing destroys every legitimate foundation for the circulation of words, for the relationship between the effects of language and the positions of bodies in shared space. Plato thereby singles out two main models, two major forms of existence and of the sensible effectivity of language – writing and the theatre –, which are also structure-giving forms for the regime of the arts in general. However, these forms turn out to be prejudicially linked from the outset to a certain regime of politics, a regime based on the indetermination of identities, the delegitimation of positions of speech, the deregulation of partitions of space and time. This aesthetic regime of politics is strictly identical with the regime of democracy, the regime based on the assembly of artisans, inviolable written laws, and the theatre as institution. Plato contrasts a third, good *form of art* with writing and the theatre, the *choreographic* form of the community that sings and dances its own proper unity. In sum, Plato singles out three ways in which discursive and bodily practices suggest forms of community: the surface of mute signs that are, he says, [16] like paintings, and the space of bodily movement that divides itself into two antagonistic models (the movement of simulacra on the stage that is offered as material for the audience's identifications and, on the other hand, the authentic movement characteristic of communal bodies).

Here we have three ways of distributing the sensible that structure the manner in which the arts can be perceived and thought of as forms of art *and* as forms that inscribe a sense of community: the surface of 'depicted' signs, the split reality of the theatre, the rhythm of a dancing chorus. These forms define the way in which works of art or performances are 'involved in politics', whatever may otherwise be the guiding intentions, artists' social modes of integration, or the manner in which artistic forms reflect social structures or movements. When *Madame Bovary* was published, or *Sentimental Education*, these works were immediately perceived as 'democracy in literature' despite Flaubert's aristocratic situation and political conformism. His very refusal to entrust literature with any message whatsoever was considered to be evidence of democratic equality. His adversaries claimed that he was [17] democratic due to his decision to depict and portray instead of instruct. This equality of indifference is the result of a poetic bias: the equality of all subject matter is the negation of any relationship of necessity between a determined form and a determined content. Yet what is this indifference after all if not the very equality of everything that comes to pass on a written page, available as it is to everyone's eyes? This equality destroys all of the hierarchies of representation and also establishes a community of readers as a community without legitimacy, a community formed only by the random circulation of the written word.

In this way, a sensible politicity exists that is immediately attributed to the major forms of aesthetic distribution such as the theatre, the page, or the chorus. These 'politics' obey their own proper logic, and they offer their services in very different contexts and time periods. Consider the way these paradigms functioned in the connection between art and politics at the end of the nineteenth century and the beginning of the twentieth. Consider, for example, the role taken on by the paradigm of the page in all its different forms, which exceed the materiality of a written sheet of paper. Novelistic democracy, on the one hand, is the indifferent democracy of writing such as [18] it is symbolized by the novel and its readership. There is also, however, the knowledge concerning typography and iconography, the intertwining of graphic and pictorial capabilities, that played such an important role in the Renaissance and was revived by Romantic typography through its use of vignettes, culs-de-lampe, and various innovations. This model disturbs the clear-cut rules of representative logic that establish a relationship of correspondence at a distance between the sayable and the visible. It also disturbs the clear partition between works of pure art and the ornaments made by the decorative arts. This is why it played such an important – and generally underestimated – role in the upheaval of the representative paradigm and of its political implications. I am thinking in particular of its role in the Arts and Crafts movement and all of its derivatives (Art Deco, Bauhaus, Constructivism). These movements developed an idea of furniture – in the broad sense of the term – for a new community, which also inspired a new idea of pictorial surface as a surface of shared writing.

Modernist discourse presents the revolution of pictorial abstraction as painting's discovery of its own proper 'medium': two-dimensional surface. By revoking the perspectivist illusion of the third dimension, painting was to regain [19] the mastery of its own proper surface. In actual fact, however, this surface does not have any distinctive feature. A 'surface' is not simply a geometric composition of lines. It is a certain distribution of the sensible. For Plato, writing and painting were equivalent surfaces of mute signs, deprived of the breath that animates and transports living speech. Flat surfaces, in this logic, are not opposed to depth in the sense of three-dimensional surfaces. They are opposed to the 'living'. The mute surface of depicted signs stands in opposition to the act of 'living' speech, which is guided by the speaker towards its appropriate addressee. Moreover, painting's adoption of the third dimension was also a response to this distribution. The reproduction of optical depth was linked to the privilege accorded to the *story*. In the Renaissance, the reproduction of three-dimensional space was involved in the valorization of painting and the assertion of its ability to capture an act of living speech, the decisive moment of action and meaning. In opposition to the Platonic degradation of *mimēsis*, the classical poetics of representation wanted to endow the 'flat surface' with speech or with a 'scene' of life, with a specific depth such as the manifestation of an action, the expression of an interiority, or the transmission of meaning. Classical poetics established [20] a relationship of correspondence at a distance between speech and painting, between the sayable and the visible, which gave 'imitation' its own specific space.

It is this relationship that is at stake in the supposed distinction between two-dimensional and three-dimensional space as 'specific' to a particular form of art. To a large extent, the ground was laid for painting's 'anti-representative revolution' by the flat surface of the page, in the change in how literature's 'images' function or the change in the discourse on painting, but also in the ways in which typography, posters, and the decorative arts became interlaced. The type of painting that is poorly named abstract, and which is supposedly brought back to its own proper medium, is implicated in an overall vision of a new human being lodged in new structures, surrounded by different objects. Its flatness is linked to the flatness of pages, posters, and tapestries. It is the flatness of an interface. Moreover, its anti-representative 'purity' is inscribed in a context where pure art and decorative art are intertwined, a context that straight away gives it a political signification. This context is not the surrounding revolutionary fever that made Malevich at once the artist who painted *Black Square* and the revolutionary eulogist of [21] 'new forms of life'. Furthermore, this is not some theatrical ideal of the new human being that seals the momentary alliance between revolutionary artists and politics. It is initially in the interface created between different 'mediums' – in the connections forged between poems and their typography or their illustrations, between the theatre and its set designers or poster designers, between decorative objects and poems – that this 'newness' is formed that links the artist who abolishes figurative representation to the revolutionary who invents a new form of life. This interface is political in that it revokes the twofold politics inherent in the logic of representation. On the one hand, this logic separated the world of artistic imitations from the world of vital concerns and politico-social grandeur. On the other hand, its hierarchical organization – in particular the primacy of living speech/action over depicted images – formed an analogy with the socio-political order. With the triumph of the novel's page over the theatrical stage, the egalitarian intertwining of images and signs on pictorial or typographic surfaces, the elevation of artisans' art to the status of great art, and the new claim to bring art into the décor of each and every life, an entire well-ordered distribution of sensory experience was overturned.

[22] This is how the 'planarity' of the surface of depicted signs, the form of egalitarian distribution of the sensible stigmatized by Plato, intervened as the principle behind an art's 'formal' revolution at the same time as the principle behind the political redistribution of shared experience. The other major forms, among which there are those of the chorus and the theatre that I mentioned earlier, could be considered in much the same way. A history of aesthetic politics, understood in this sense, has to take into account the way in which these major forms stand in opposition to one another or intermingle. I am thinking, for example, of the way in which this paradigm of the surface of signs/forms entered into conflict or joined forces with the theatrical paradigm of presence, and with the diverse forms that this paradigm itself has taken on, from the Symbolist figuration of a collective legend to the actualized chorus of a new humanity. Politics plays itself out in the theatrical paradigm as the relationship between the stage and the audience, as meaning produced by the actor's body, as games of proximity or distance. Mallarmé's critical prose writings stage, in an exemplary manner, the play of cross-references, oppositions or assimilations between these forms, from the intimate theatre of the page or calligraphic choreography to the new 'service' performed by concerts.

[23] In one respect, these forms therefore appear to bring forth, in very different contexts, figures of community equal to themselves. However, they are susceptible to being assigned to contradictory political paradigms. Let us take the example of the tragic stage. It simultaneously carries with it, according to Plato, the syndrome of democracy and the power of illusion. By isolating *mimēsis* in its own proper space

and by enclosing tragedy within a logic of genres, Aristotle – even if this was not his intention – redefined its politicity. Furthermore, in the classical system of representation, the tragic stage would become the stage of visibility for an orderly world governed by a hierarchy of subject matter and the adaptation of situations and manners of speaking to this hierarchy. The democratic paradigm would become a monarchical paradigm. Let us also consider the long and contradictory history of rhetoric and the model of the 'good orator'. Throughout the monarchical age, democratic eloquence à la Demosthenes denoted an excellence in speaking, which was itself established as the imaginary attribute of the supreme power. It was also always receptive, however, to the recovery of its democratic function by lending its [24] canonical forms and its consecrated images to the transgressive appearance of unauthorized speakers on the public stage. Let us consider as well the contradictory destinies of the choreographic model. Recent research has evoked the metamorphoses undergone by Laban's notation of movement. It was developed in a context favouring the liberation of bodies and became the model for the large Nazi demonstrations before regaining, in the anti-establishment context of performance art, a new subversive virginity. Benjamin's explanation via the fatal aestheticization of politics in the 'era of the masses' overlooks, perhaps, the long-standing connection between the unanimous consensus of the citizenry and the exaltation of the free movement of bodies. In a city hostile to the theatre and to written law, Plato recommended constantly cradling unweaned infants.

I have evoked these three forms because Plato conceptually charted them out and because they maintain a historical constancy. They obviously do not define all of the ways that figures of community are aesthetically designed. The important thing is that the question of the relationship between aesthetics and politics be raised at this level, the level of the sensible delimitation of what is common to the community, the forms of its visibility and of its organization. [25] It is from this perspective that it is possible to reflect on artists' political interventions, starting with the Romantic literary forms that aimed at deciphering society, the Symbolist poetics of dreams or the Dadaist or Constructivist elimination of art, and continuing up to the contemporary modes of performance and installation. From this perspective, it is possible to challenge a good many imaginary stories about artistic 'modernity' and vain debates over the autonomy of art or its submission to politics. The arts only ever lend to projects of domination or emancipation what they are able to lend to them, that is to say, quite simply, what they have in common with them: bodily positions and movements, functions of speech, the parcelling out of the visible and the invisible. Furthermore, the autonomy they can enjoy or the subversion they can claim credit for rest on the same foundation.

Artistic Regimes and the Shortcomings of the Notion of Modernity

Certain of the most fundamental categories used for thinking about artistic creation in the twentieth century, namely the categories of modernity, the avant-garde and, for some time now, postmodernity, also happen to have a political meaning. Do these categories seem to you to have the slightest interest for conceiving, in precise terms, what ties 'aesthetics' to 'politics'?

I do not think that the notions of modernity and the avant-garde have been very enlightening when it comes to thinking about the new forms of art that have emerged since the last century or the relations between aesthetics and politics. They actually confuse two very different things: the historicity specific to a regime of the arts in general and the decisions to break with the past or anticipate the future that take place within this regime. The notion of aesthetic modernity conceals – without conceptualizing it in the least – the singularity of a particular regime of the arts, that is [27] to say of a specific type of connection between ways of producing works of art or developing practices, forms of visibility that disclose them, and ways of conceptualizing the former and the latter.

A detour is necessary here in order to clarify this notion and situate the problem. With regard to what we call *art*, it is in fact possible to distinguish, within the Western tradition, three major regimes of identification. There is first of all what I propose to call an ethical regime of images. In this regime, 'art' is not identified as such but is subsumed under the question of images. As a specific type of entity, images are the object of a twofold question: the question of their origin (and consequently their truth content) and the question of their end or purpose, the uses they are put to and the effects they result in. The question of images of the divine and the right to produce such images or the ban placed on them falls within this regime, as well as the question of the status and signification of the images produced. The entire Platonic polemic against the simulacra of painting, poems, and the stage also falls within this regime.[6] Plato does not, as it is often claimed, place art under the yoke of politics. This very distinction would have made no sense for Plato since art did not exist for [28] him but only arts, ways of doing and making. And it is among these that he traces the dividing line: there are true arts, that is to say forms of knowledge based on the imitation of a model with precise ends, and artistic simulacra that imitate simple appearances. These imitations, differentiated by their origin, are then distinguished by their end or purpose, by the way in which the poem's images provide the spectators, both children and adult citizens, with a certain education and fit in with the distribution of the city's occupations. It is in this sense that I speak of an ethical regime of images. In this regime, it is a matter of knowing in what way images' mode of being affects the *ethos*, the mode of being of individuals and communities. This question prevents 'art' from individualizing itself as such.[7]

The poetic – or representative – regime of the arts breaks away from the ethical regime of images. It identifies the substance of art – or rather of the arts – in the couple *poiēis/mimēsis*. The mimetic principle is not at its core a normative principle stating that art must make copies resembling their models. It is first of all a pragmatic principle that isolates, within the general domain of the arts (ways of doing and making), certain particular forms of art that produce specific entities [29] called imitations. These imitations are extricated, at one and the same time, from the ordinary control of artistic products by their use and from the legislative reign of truth over discourses and images. Such is the vast operation carried out by the Aristotelian elaboration of *mimēsis* and by the privilege accorded to tragic action. It is the *substance* of the poem, the fabrication of a plot arranging actions that represent the activities of men, which is the foremost issue, to the detriment of the *essence* of the image, a copy examined with regard to its model. Such is the principle guiding the functional change in the theatrical model I was speaking of earlier. The principle regulating the external delimitation of a well-founded domain of imitations is thus at the same time a normative principle of inclusion. It develops into forms of normativity that define the conditions according to which imitations can be recognized as exclusively belonging to an art and assessed, within this framework, as good or bad, adequate or inadequate: partitions between the representable and the unrepresentable; the distinction between genres according to what is represented; principles for adapting forms of expression to genres and thus to the subject matter represented; the distribution of resemblances [30] according to principles of verisimilitude, appropriateness, or correspondence; criteria for distinguishing between and comparing the arts; etc.

I call this regime *poetic* in the sense that it identifies the arts – what the Classical Age would later call the 'fine arts' – within a classification of ways of doing and making, and it consequently defines proper ways of doing and making as well as means of assessing imitations. I call it *representative* insofar as it is the notion of representation or *mimēsis* that organizes these ways of doing, making, seeing, and judging. Once again, however, *mimēsis* is not the law that brings the arts under the yoke of resemblance. It is first of all a fold in the distribution of ways of doing and making as well as in social occupations, a fold that renders the arts visible. It is not an artistic process but a regime of visibility regarding the arts. A regime of visibility is at once what renders the arts autonomous and also what links this autonomy to a general order of occupations and ways of doing and making. This is what I evoked earlier concerning the logic of representation, which enters into a relationship of global analogy with an overall hierarchy of political and social occupations. The representative primacy of action over characters or of narration over [31] description, the hierarchy of genres according to the dignity of their subject matter, and the very primacy of the art of speaking, of speech in actuality, all of these elements figure into an analogy with a fully hierarchical vision of the community.

The aesthetic regime of the arts stands in contrast with the representative regime. I call this regime *aesthetic* because the identification of art no longer occurs via a division within ways of doing and making, but it is based on distinguishing a sensible mode of being specific to artistic products. The word aesthetics does not refer to a theory of sensibility, taste, and pleasure for art amateurs. It strictly refers to the specific mode of being of whatever falls within the domain of art, to the mode of being of the objects of art. In the aesthetic regime, artistic phenomena are identified by their adherence to a specific regime of the sensible, which is extricated from its ordinary connections and is inhabited by a heterogeneous power, the power of a form of thought that has become foreign to itself: a product identical with something not produced, knowledge transformed into non-knowledge, *logos* identical with pathos, the intention of the unintentional, etc. This idea of a regime of the sensible that has become foreign to itself, the locus for a form of thought that has become foreign to itself, is the invariable core in the [32] identifications of art that have configured the aesthetic mode of thought from the outset: Vico's discovery of the 'true Homer' as a poet in spite of himself, Kantian 'genius' that is unaware of the law it produces, Schiller's 'aesthetic state' that suspends both the activity of the understanding and sensible passivity, Schelling's definition of art as the identity between a conscious process and an unconscious process, etc. The aesthetic mode of thought likewise runs through the specific definitions that the arts have given to themselves in the Modern Age: Proust's idea of a book that would be entirely planned out and fully removed from the realm of the will; Mallarmé's idea of a poem by the spectator-poet, written 'without the scribe's apparatus' by the steps of an illiterate dancer; the Surrealist practice of producing work that expresses the artist's unconscious with the outdated illustrations in catalogues or newspaper serials from the previous century; Bresson's idea of film as the film-maker's thought withdrawn from the body of the 'models' who, by unthinkingly repeating the words and gestures he lays down for them, manifest their proper truth without either the film-maker or the models knowing it; etc.

It is pointless to go on with definitions and examples. We need to indicate, on the contrary, the heart of the problem. The aesthetic regime [33] of the arts is the regime that strictly identifies art in the singular and frees it from any specific rule, from any hierarchy of the arts, subject matter, and genres. Yet it does so by destroying the mimetic barrier that distinguished ways of doing and making affiliated with art from other ways of doing and making, a barrier that separated its rules from the order of social occupations. The aesthetic regime asserts the absolute singularity of art and, at the same time, destroys any pragmatic criterion for isolating this singularity. It simultaneously establishes the autonomy of art and the identity of its forms with the forms that life uses to shape itself. Schiller's *aesthetic state*, which is this regime's first manifesto (and remains, in a sense, unsurpassable), clearly indicates this fundamental identity of opposites. The aesthetic state is a pure instance of suspension, a moment when form is experienced for itself. Moreover, it is the moment of the formation and education of a specific type of humanity.

From this perspective, it is possible to understand the functions served by the notion of modernity. The aesthetic regime of the arts, it can be said, is the true name for what is designated by the incoherent label 'modernity'. However, 'modernity' is more than an incoherent label. It is, in its different versions, the concept that diligently works at [34] masking the specificity of this regime of the arts and the very meaning of the specificity of regimes of art. It traces, in order either to exalt or deplore it, a simple line of transition or rupture between the old and the new, the representative and the non-representative or the anti-representative. The basis for this simplistic historical account was the transition to non-figurative representation in painting. This transition was theorized by being cursorily assimilated into artistic 'modernity's' overall anti-mimetic destiny. When the eulogists of this form of modernity saw the exhibition-spaces for the well-behaved destiny of modernity invaded by all kinds of objects, machines, and unidentified devices, they began denouncing the 'tradition of the new', a desire for innovation that would reduce artistic modernity to the emptiness of its self-declaration. However, it is the starting point that is erroneous. The leap outside of *mimēsis* is by no means the refusal of figurative representation. Furthermore, its inaugural moment has often been called *realism*, which does not in any way mean the valorization of resemblance but rather the destruction of the structures within which it functioned. Thus, novelistic realism is first of all the reversal of the hierarchies of representation (the primacy of the narrative over the descriptive [35] or the hierarchy of subject matter) and the adoption of a fragmented or proximate mode of focalization, which imposes raw presence to the detriment of the rational sequences of the story. The aesthetic regime of the arts does not contrast the old with the new. It contrasts, more profoundly, two regimes of historicity. It is within the mimetic regime that the old stands in contrast with the new. In the aesthetic regime of art, the future of art, its separation from the present of non-art, incessantly restages the past.

Those who exalt or denounce the 'tradition of the new' actually forget that this tradition has as its strict complement the 'newness of the tradition'. The aesthetic regime of the arts did not begin with decisions to initiate an artistic rupture. It began with decisions to reinterpret what makes art or what art makes: Vico discovering the 'true Homer', that is to say not an inventor of fables and characters but a witness to the image-laden language and thought of ancient times; Hegel indicating the true subject matter of Dutch genre painting: not in stories or descriptions of interiors but a nation's freedom displayed in reflections of light; Hölderlin reinventing Greek tragedy; Balzac [36] contrasting the poetry of the geologist who reconstructs worlds out of tracks and fossils with the poetry that makes do with reproducing a bit of agitation in the soul; Mendelssohn replaying the *St. Matthew Passion*; etc. The aesthetic regime of the arts is first of all a new regime for relating to the past. It actually sets up as the very principle of artisticity the expressive relationship inherent in a time and a state of civilization, a relationship that was previously considered to be the 'non-artistic' part of works of art (the part that was excused by invoking the crudeness of the times when the author lived). The aesthetic regime of the arts invents its revolutions on the basis of the same idea that caused it to invent the museum and art history, the notion of classicism and new forms of reproduction… And it devotes itself to the invention of new forms of life on the basis of an idea of what art *was*, an idea of what art *would have been*. When the Futurists or the Constructivists declared the end of art and the identification of its practices with the practices that construct, decorate, or give a certain rhythm to the times and spaces of communal life, they proposed an end of art equivalent to the identification of art with the life of the community. This proposal is directly dependent on the Schillerian and Romantic reinterpretation of Greek art as a community's mode of life, while also communicating, [37] in other respects, with the new styles introduced by the inventors of advertising who, for their part, did not propose a revolution but only a new way of living amongst words, images, and commodities. The idea of modernity is a questionable notion that tries to make clear-cut distinctions in the complex configuration of the aesthetic regime of the arts. It tries to retain the forms of rupture, the iconoclastic gestures, etc., by separating them from the context that allows for their

existence: history, interpretation, patrimony, the museum, the pervasiveness of reproduction... The idea of modernity would like there to
be only one meaning and direction in history, whereas the temporality
specific to the aesthetic regime of the arts is a co-presence of heterogeneous temporalities.

The notion of modernity thus seems to have been deliberately
invented to prevent a clear understanding of the transformations of
art and its relationships with the other spheres of collective experience.
The confusion introduced by this notion has, it seems to me, two
major forms. Both of them, without analysing it, rely on the contradiction constitutive of the aesthetic regime of the arts, which makes art
into an *autonomous form of life* and thereby sets down, at one and the
same time, the autonomy of art and its identification with a moment
in life's process of self-formation. The two [38] major variants of the
discourse on 'modernity' derive from this contradiction. The first
variant would have modernity identified simply with the autonomy
of art, an 'anti-mimetic' revolution in art identical with the conquest
of the pure form of art finally laid bare. Each individual art would
thus assert the pure potential of art by exploring the capabilities of
its specific medium. Poetic or literary modernity would explore the
capabilities of a language diverted from its communicational uses.
Pictorial modernity would bring painting back to its distinctive feature:
coloured pigment and a two-dimensional surface. Musical modernity
would be identified with the language of twelve sounds, set free from
any analogy with expressive language, etc. Furthermore, these specific
forms of modernity would be in a relationship of distant analogy with
a political modernity susceptible to being identified, depending on the
time period, with revolutionary radicality or with the sober and disenchanted modernity of good republican government. The main feature
of what is called the 'crisis of art' is the overwhelming defeat of this
simple modernist paradigm, which is forever more distant from the
mixtures of genres and mediums as well as from the numerous political
possibilities inherent in the arts' contemporary forms. [39]

This overwhelming defeat is obviously overdetermined by the
modernist paradigm's second major form, which might be called
modernatism. I mean by this the identification of forms from the
aesthetic regime of the arts with forms that accomplish a task or fulfil

a destiny specific to modernity. At the root of this identification there is a specific interpretation of the structural and generative contradiction of aesthetic 'form'. It is, in this case, the determination of art qua form and self-formation of life that is valorized. The starting point, Schiller's notion of the *aesthetic education of man*, constitutes an unsurpassable reference point. It is this notion that established the idea that domination and servitude are, in the first place, part of an ontological distribution (the activity of thought versus the passivity of sensible matter). It is also this notion that defined a neutral state, a state of dual cancellation, where the activity of thought and sensible receptivity become a single reality. They constitute a sort of new region of being – the region of free play and appearance – that makes it possible to conceive of the equality whose direct materialization, according to Schiller, was shown to be impossible by the French Revolution. It is this specific mode of living in the sensible world that must be developed by 'aesthetic education' [40] in order to train men susceptible to live in a free political community. The idea of modernity as a time devoted to the material realization of a humanity still latent in mankind was constructed on this foundation. It can be said, regarding this point, that the 'aesthetic revolution' produced a new idea of political revolution: the material realization of a common humanity still only existing as an idea. This is how Schiller's 'aesthetic state' became the 'aesthetic programme' of German Romanticism, the programme summarized in the rough draft written together by Hegel, Hölderlin, and Schelling: the material realization of unconditional freedom and pure thought in common forms of life and belief. It is this paradigm of aesthetic autonomy that became the new paradigm for revolution, and it subsequently allowed for the brief but decisive encounter between the artisans of the Marxist revolution and the artisans of forms for a new way of life. The failure of this revolution determined the destiny – in two phases – of modernatism. At first, artistic modernatism, in its authentic revolutionary potential for [41] hope and defiance, was set against the degeneration of political revolution. Surrealism and the Frankfurt School were the principal vehicles for this counter-modernity. The failure of political revolution was later conceived of as the failure of its ontologico-aesthetic model. Modernity thus became something like a fatal destiny based on a fundamental forgetting:

the essence of technology according to Heidegger, the revolutionary severing of the king's head as a severing of tradition in the history of humanity, and finally the original sin of human beings, forgetful of their debt to the Other and of their submission to the heterogeneous powers of the sensible.

What is called *postmodernism* is really the process of this reversal. At first, postmodernism brought to light everything in the recent evolution of the arts and possible ways of thinking the arts that destroyed modernism's theoretical edifice: the crossing-over and mixture between the arts that destroyed Lessing's conventional set of principles concerning the separation of the arts; the collapse of the paradigm of functionalist architecture and the return of the curved line and embellishment; the breakdown of the pictorial/two-dimensional/abstract model through the return of figurative representation and [42] signification as well as the slow invasion of painting's exhibition-space by three-dimensional and narrative forms, from Pop Art to installation art and 'rooms' for video art;[8] the new combinations of painting and language as well as of monumental sculpture and the projection of shadows and lights; the break-up of the serial tradition through new mixtures between musical systems, genres, and epochs. The teleological model of modernity became untenable at the same time as its divisions between the 'distinctive features' of the different arts, or the separation of a pure domain of art. Postmodernism, in a sense, was simply the name under whose guise certain artists and thinkers realized what modernism had been: a desperate attempt to establish a 'distinctive feature of art' by linking it to a simple teleology of historical evolution and rupture. There was not really a need, moreover, to make this late recognition of a fundamental fact of the aesthetic regime of the arts into an actual temporal break, the real end of a historical period.

However, it was precisely the next episode that showed that postmodernism was more than this. The joyful, postmodern artistic license, its [43] exaltation of the carnival of simulacra, all sorts of interbreeding and hybridization, transformed very quickly and came to challenge the freedom or autonomy that the modernatist principle conferred – or would have conferred – upon art the mission of accomplishing. There was thus a return from the carnival to the primal scene. However, the primal scene can be taken in two senses, either as the starting point of a process or as an original separation. Modernist faith had latched on to the idea of the 'aesthetic education of man' that Schiller had extracted from the Kantian analytic of the beautiful. The postmodern reversal had as its theoretical foundation Lyotard's analysis of the Kantian sublime, which was reinterpreted as the scene of a founding distance separating the idea from any sensible presentation. From this moment onward, postmodernism came into harmony with the mourning and repenting of modernatist thought, and the scene of sublime distance came to epitomize all sorts of scenes of original distance or original sin: the Heideggerian flight of the gods, the irreducible aspect of the unsymbolizable object and the death drive as analysed by Freud, the voice of the Absolutely Other declaring a ban on representation, the revolutionary murder of the Father. Postmodernism thus became the grand threnody of the unrepresentable/intractable[44]/irredeemable, denouncing the modern madness of the idea of a self-emancipation of mankind's humanity and its inevitable and interminable culmination in the death camps.

The notion of the avant-garde defines the type of subject suitable to the modernist vision and appropriate, according to this vision, for connecting the aesthetic to the political. Its success is due less to the convenient connection it proposes between the artistic idea of innovation and the idea of politically-guided change, than to the more covert connection it establishes between two ideas of the 'avant-garde'. On the one hand, there is the topographical and military notion of the force that marches in the lead, that has a clear understanding of the movement, embodies its forces, determines the direction of historical evolution, and chooses subjective political orientations.[9] In short, there is the idea that links political subjectivity to a certain form: the party, an advanced detachment that derives its ability to lead from its ability to read and interpret the signs of history. On the other hand, there is another idea of the avant-garde that, in accordance with Schiller's model, is rooted in the aesthetic anticipation of the future. If the concept of the avant-garde has any meaning in the aesthetic regime of the arts, it is on this side of things, not on the side of the [45] advanced detachments of artistic innovation but on the side of the invention of sensible forms and material structures for a life to come. This is what the 'aesthetic' avant-garde brought to the 'political' avant-garde, or what it wanted to bring to it – and what it believed to have brought to it – by transforming politics into a total life programme. The history of the relations between political parties and aesthetic movements is first of all the history of a confusion, sometimes complacently maintained, at other times violently denounced, between these two ideas of the avant-garde, which are in fact two different ideas of political subjectivity: the archi-political idea of a party, that is to say the idea of a form of political intelligence that sums up the essential conditions for change, and the meta-political idea of global political subjectivity, the idea of the potentiality inherent in the innovative sensible modes of experience that anticipate a community to come. There is, however, nothing accidental about this confusion. It is not the case, as today's doxa would have us believe, that artists' ambitious claims to a total revolution of the sensible paved the way for totalitarianism. It is rather that the very idea of a political avant-garde is divided between the strategic conception and the aesthetic conception of the avant-garde. [46]

Mechanical Arts and the Promotion of the Anonymous

In one of your texts, you establish a connection between the development of photography and film as 'mechanical' arts and the birth of 'new history'.[10] Can you explain this connection? Does it correspond to Benjamin's idea that the masses as such acquired visibility at the beginning of the century with the help of the 'mechanical' arts?

Perhaps first I should clear up a misunderstanding concerning the notion of 'mechanical arts'. The connection I established was between a scientific paradigm and an *aesthetic* paradigm. Benjamin's thesis presupposes something different, which seems questionable to me: the deduction of the aesthetic and political properties of a form of art from its technical properties. Mechanical arts, qua *mechanical* arts, would result in a change of artistic paradigm and a new relationship between art and [47] its subject matter. This proposition refers back to one of modernism's main theses: the difference between the arts is linked to the difference between their technological conditions or their specific medium or material. This assimilation can be understood either in the simple modernist mode, or in accordance with modernatist hyperbole. The persistent success of Benjamin's theses on art in the age of mechanical reproduction is, moreover, undoubtedly due to the crossing-over they allow for between the categories of Marxist materialist explanation and those of Heideggerian ontology, which ascribe the age of modernity to the unfurling of the essence of technology. This link between the aesthetic and the onto-technological has, in fact, been subjected to the general fate of modernist categories. In Benjamin, Duchamp, or Rodchenko's time, it coexisted with the faith in the capabilities of electricity and machines, iron, glass, and concrete. With the so-called 'postmodern' reversal, it has kept pace with the return to the icon, which presents the veil of Veronica as the essence of painting, film, or photography.

It is thus necessary, in my opinion, to take things the other way around. In order for the mechanical arts to be able to confer visibility on the masses, or rather on anonymous individuals, they [48] first need to be recognized as arts. That is to say that they first need to be put into practice and recognized as something other than techniques of reproduction or transmission. It is thus the same principle that confers visibility on absolutely anyone and allows for photography and film to become arts. We can even reverse the formula: it is because the anonymous became the subject matter of art that the act of recording such a subject matter can be an art. The fact that what is anonymous is not only susceptible to becoming the subject matter of art but also conveys a specific beauty is an exclusive characteristic of the aesthetic regime of the arts. Not only did the aesthetic regime begin well before the arts of mechanical reproduction, but it is actually this regime that made them possible by its new way of thinking art and its subject matter.

The aesthetic regime of the arts was initially the breakdown of the system of representation, that is to say of a system where the dignity of the subject matter dictated the dignity of genres of representation (tragedy for the nobles, comedy for the people of meagre means; historical painting versus genre painting; etc.). Along with genres, the system of representation defined the situations and forms of expression that were appropriate for the lowliness or loftiness of the subject matter. The aesthetic regime [49] of the arts dismantled this correlation between subject matter and mode of representation. This revolution first took place in literature: an epoch and a society were deciphered through the features, clothes, or gestures of an ordinary individual (Balzac); the sewer revealed a civilization (Hugo); the daughter of a farmer and the daughter of a banker were caught in the equal force of style as an 'absolute manner of seeing things' (Flaubert). All of these forms of cancellation or reversal of the opposition between high and low not only antedate the powers of mechanical reproduction, they made it possible for this reproduction to be more than mechanical reproduction. In order for a technological mode of action and production, i.e. a way of doing and making, to be qualified as falling within the domain of art – be it a certain use of words or of a camera –, it is first necessary for its subject matter to be defined as such. Photography was not established as an art on the grounds of its technological nature. The discourse on the originality of photography as an 'indexical' art is very recent, and it is less a part of the history of photography than of the history of the postmodern reversal touched upon above.[11] Furthermore, photography did not become an art by imitating the mannerisms of art. Benjamin accurately demonstrated this regarding [50] David Octavius Hill: it is with the little anonymous fishwife from New Haven, not with his grand pictorial compositions, that he brought photography into the world of art. Likewise, it is not the ethereal subject matter and soft focus of pictorialism that secured the status of photographic art, it is rather the appropriation of the commonplace: the emigrants in Stieglitz's *The Steerage*, the frontal portraits by Paul Strand or Walker Evans.[12] On the one hand, the technological revolution comes after the aesthetic revolution. On the other hand, however, the aesthetic revolution is first of all the honour acquired by the commonplace, which is pictorial and literary before being photographic or cinematic.

We should add that the honour conferred on the commonplace is part of the science of literature before being part of the science of history. Film and photography did not determine the subject matter and modes of focalization of 'new history'. On the contrary, the new science of history and the arts of mechanical reproduction are inscribed in the same logic of aesthetic revolution. This programme is literary before being scientific: it shifts the focus from great names and events to the life of the anonymous; it finds symptoms of an epoch, a society, or a civilization in the minute details of ordinary life [51]; it explains the surface by subterranean layers; and it reconstructs worlds from their vestiges. This does not simply mean that the science of history has a literary prehistory. Literature itself was constituted as a kind of symptomatology of society, and it set this symptomatology in contrast with the clamour and imagination of the public stage. In his preface to *Cromwell*, Hugo called for a literature based on the story of the customs of everyday life that would be opposed to the story of events practised by historians. In *War and Peace*, Tolstoy contrasted the documents of literature, taken from narratives and testimonial accounts of the action of innumerable anonymous actors, with the documents of historians, taken from the archives – and from the imagination – of those who believe to have been in charge of battles and to have made history. Scholarly history took over this opposition when it contrasted the history of the lifestyles of the masses and the cycles of material life based on reading and interpreting 'mute witnesses' with the former history of princes, battles, and treaties based on courts' chronicles and diplomatic reports. The appearance of the masses [52] on the scene of history or in 'new' images is not to be confused with the link between the age of the masses and the age of science and technology. It is first and foremost rooted in the aesthetic logic of a mode of visibility that, on the one hand, revokes the representative tradition's scales of grandeur and, on the other hand, revokes the oratorical model of speech in favour of the interpretation of signs on the body of people, things, and civilizations.[13]

This is what scholarly history inherited. However, its intention was to separate the condition of its new object (the life of the anonymous) from its literary origin and from the politics of literature in which it is inscribed. What it cast aside – which was reappropriated by film and photography – was the logic revealed by the tradition of the novel (from Balzac to Proust and Surrealism) and the reflection on the true that Marx, Freud, Benjamin, and the tradition of 'critical thought' inherited: the ordinary becomes beautiful as a trace of the true. And the ordinary becomes a trace of the true if it is torn from its obviousness in order to become a hieroglyph, a mythological or phantasmagoric figure. This phantasmagoric dimension of the true, which belongs to the aesthetic regime of the arts, played an essential role in the formation of the critical paradigm of the human and social sciences. [53] The Marxist theory of fetishism is the most striking testimony to this fact: commodities must be torn out of their trivial appearances, made into phantasmagoric objects in order to be interpreted as the expression of society's contradictions. Scholarly history tried to separate out various features within the aesthetico-political configuration that gave it its object. It flattened this phantasmagoria of the true into the positivist sociological concepts of mentality/expression and belief/ignorance. [54]

Is History a Form of Fiction?[14]

You refer to the idea of fiction as essentially belonging to the domain of empirical reality. How exactly is this to be understood? What are the connections between the History we are 'involved' in and the stories told (or deconstructed) by the narrative arts? And how are we to make sense of the fact that poetic or literary locutions 'take shape', have real effects, rather than being reflections of the real? Are the concepts of 'political bodies' or a 'communal body' more than metaphors? Does this reflection involve a redefinition of utopia?

There are two problems here that certain people confuse in order to construct the phantom of a historical reality that would solely be made up of 'fictions'. The first problem concerns the relationship between history and historicity, that is to say the relationship of the historical agent to the speaking being. The second problem concerns the idea of fiction and the relationship between [55] fictional rationality and the modes of explanation used for historical and social reality, the relationship between the logic of fiction and the logic of facts.

It is preferable to begin with the second problem, the 'actuality' of fiction analysed by the text you refer to.[15] This actuality itself raises a twofold question: the general question of fiction's rationality, i.e. the distinction between fiction and falsity, and the question of the distinction – or the indistinction – between the modes of intelligibility specific to the construction of stories and the modes of intelligibility used for understanding historical phenomena. Let's start from the beginning. The specificity of the representative regime of the arts is characterized by the separation between the idea of fiction and that of lies. It is this regime that confers autonomy on the arts' various forms in relationship to the economy of communal occupations and the counter-economy of simulacra specific to the ethical regime of images. This is what is essentially at stake in Aristotle's *Poetics*, which safeguards the forms of poetic *mimēsis* from the Platonic suspicion concerning what images consist of and their end or purpose. The *Poetics* declares that the arrangement of a poem's actions is not equivalent to the fabrication of a simulacrum.[16] It is a play of [56] knowledge that is carried out in a determined space-time. To pretend is not to put forth illusions but to elaborate intelligible structures. Poetry owes no explanation for the 'truth' of what it says because, in its very principle, it is not made up of images or statements, but fictions, that is to say arrangements between actions. The other consequence that Aristotle derives from this is the superiority of poetry, which confers a causal logic on the arrangement of events, over history, condemned to presenting events according to their empirical disorder. In other words – and this is obviously something that historians do not like to examine too closely – the clear division between reality and fiction makes a rational logic of history impossible as well as a science of history.

The aesthetic revolution rearranges the rules of the game by making two things interdependent: the blurring of the borders between the logic of facts and the logic of fictions *and* the new mode of rationality that characterizes the science of history. By declaring that the principle of poetry is not to be found in fiction but in a certain arrangement of the signs of language, the Romantic Age blurred the dividing line that isolated art from the jurisdiction of statements or images, as well as the dividing line that separated the [57] logic of facts from the logic of stories. It is not the case, as is sometimes said, that it consecrated the 'autotelism' of language, separated from reality. It is the exact opposite. The Romantic Age actually plunged language into the materiality of the traits by which the historical and social world becomes visible to itself, be it in the form of the silent language of things or the coded language of images. Circulation within this landscape of signs defines, moreover, the new fictionality, the new way of telling stories, which is first of all a way of assigning meaning to the 'empirical' world of lowly actions and commonplace objects. Fictional arrangement is no longer identified with the Aristotelian causal sequence of actions 'according to necessity and plausibility'. It is an arrangement of signs. However, this literary arrangement of signs is by no means the solitary self-referentiality of language. It is the identification of modes of fictional construction with means of deciphering the signs inscribed in the general aspect of a place, a group, a wall, an article of clothing, a face. It is the association between, on the one hand, accelerations or decelerations of language, its shuffling of images or sudden changes of tone, all its differences of potential between the insignificant and the overly significant or overly meaningful [58], and on the other hand, the modalities of a trip through the landscape of significant traits deposited in the topography of spaces, the physiology of social circles, the silent expression of bodies. The 'fictionality' specific to the aesthetic age is consequently distributed between two poles: the potential of meaning inherent in everything silent and the proliferation of modes of speech and levels of meaning.

The aesthetic sovereignty of literature does not therefore amount to the reign of fiction. On the contrary, it is a regime in which the logic of descriptive and narrative arrangements in fiction becomes fundamentally indistinct from the arrangements used in the description and interpretation of the phenomena of the social and historical world. When Balzac places his reader before the entwined hieroglyphics on the tottering and heteroclite façade of the house in *At the Sign of the Cat and Racket*, or has his reader enter an antique dealer's shop, with the hero of *The Magic Skin*,[17] where jumbled up together are objects both profane and sacred, uncivilized and cultured, antique and modern, that each sum up a world, when he makes Cuvier the true poet reconstructing a world from a fossil, he establishes a regime of equivalence between the signs of the new novel and those of the description or [59] interpretation of the phenomena of a civilization. He forges this new rationality of the obvious and the obscure that goes against the grand Aristotelian arrangements and that would become the new rationality for the history of material life (which stands in opposition to the histories of great names and events).

The Aristotelian dividing line between two 'stories' or 'histories' – poets' stories and the history of historians – is thereby revoked, the dividing line that not only separated reality and fiction but also empirical succession and constructed necessity. Aristotle established the superiority of poetry, recounting 'what could happen' according to the necessity or plausibility of the poetic arrangement of actions, over history, conceived of as the empirical succession of events, of 'what happened'. The aesthetic revolution drastically disrupts things: testimony and fiction come under the same regime of meaning. On the one hand, the 'empirical' bears the marks of the true in the form of traces and imprints. 'What happened' thus comes directly under a regime of truth, a regime that demonstrates the necessity behind what happened. On the other hand, 'what could happen' no longer has the autonomous and linear form [60] of the arrangement of actions. The poetic 'story' or 'history' henceforth links the realism that shows us the poetic traces inscribed directly in reality with the artificialism that assembles complex machines of understanding.

This connection was transferred from literature to the new art of narrative, film, which brought to its highest potential the double resource of the silent imprint that speaks and the montage that calculates the values of truth and the potential for producing meaning. Documentary film, film devoted to the 'real', is in this sense capable of greater fictional invention than 'fiction' film, readily devoted to a certain stereotype of actions and characters. Chris Marker's *Le Tombeau d'Alexandre* (*The Last Bolshevik*), the object of the article you refer to, fictionalizes the history of Russia from the time of the czars to the post-communist period through the destiny of a film-maker, Alexander Medvedkin. Marker does not make him into a fictional character; he does not tell fabricated stories about the USSR. He plays off of the combination of different types of traces (interviews, significant faces, archival documents, extracts from documentary and fictional films, etc.) in order to suggest possibilities for thinking [61] this story or history. The real must be fictionalized in order to be thought. This proposition should be distinguished from any discourse – positive or negative – according to which everything is 'narrative', with alternations between 'grand' narratives and 'minor' narratives. The notion of 'narrative' locks us into oppositions between the real and artifice where both the positivists and the deconstructionists are lost. It is not a matter of claiming that everything is fiction. It is a matter of stating that the fiction of the aesthetic age defined models for connecting the presentation of facts and forms of intelligibility that blurred the border between the logic of facts and the logic of fiction. Moreover, these models were taken up by historians and analysts of social reality. Writing history and writing stories come under the same regime of truth. This has nothing whatsoever to do with a thesis on the reality or unreality of things. On the contrary, it is clear that a model for the fabrication of stories is linked to a certain idea of history as common destiny, with an idea of those who 'make history', and that this inter-penetration of the logic of facts and the logic of stories is specific to an age when anyone and everyone is considered to be participating in the task of 'making' history. Thus, it is not a matter of claiming that [62] 'History' is only made up of stories that we tell ourselves, but simply that the 'logic of stories' and the ability to act as historical agents go together. Politics and art, like forms of knowledge, construct 'fictions', that is to say *material* rearrangements of signs and images, relationships between what is seen and what is said, between what is done and what can be done.

It is here that we encounter the other question that you asked, which concerns the relationship between literarity and historicity. Political statements and literary locutions produce effects in reality. They define models of speech or action but also regimes of sensible intensity. They draft maps of the visible, trajectories between the visible and the sayable, relationships between modes of being, modes of saying, and modes of doing and making. They define variations of sensible inten-sities, perceptions, and the abilities of bodies.[18] They thereby take hold of unspecified groups of people, they widen gaps, open up space for deviations, modify the speeds, the trajectories, and the ways in which groups of people adhere to a condition, react to situations, recognize their images. They reconfigure the map of the sensible by interfering with the functionality of gestures and rhythms [63] adapted to the natural cycles of production, reproduction, and submission. Man is a political animal because he is a literary animal who lets himself be diverted from his 'natural' purpose by the power of words. This *literar-ity* is at once the condition and the effect of the circulation of 'actual' literary locutions. However, these locutions take hold of bodies and divert them from their end or purpose insofar as they are not bodies in the sense of organisms, but quasi-bodies, blocks of speech circulating without a legitimate father to accompany them toward their authorized addressee. Therefore, they do not produce collective bodies. Instead, they introduce lines of fracture and disincorporation into imaginary collective bodies. This has always been, as is well known, the phobia of those in power and the theoreticians of good government, worried that the circulation of writing would produce 'disorder in the established system of classification'. It was also, in the nineteenth century, the phobia of 'actual' writers who wrote in order to denounce the literarity that overflows the institution of literature and leads its products astray. It is true that the circulation of these quasi-bodies causes modifications in the sensory perception of what is common to the community, in the relationship [64] between what is common to language and the sensible distribution of spaces and occupations. They form, in this way, uncertain communities that contribute to the formation of enunciative collectives that call into question the distribution of roles, territories, and languages. In short, they contribute to the formation of political subjects that challenge the given distribution of the sensible. A political collective is not, in actual fact, an organism or a communal body. The channels for political subjectivization are not those of imaginary identification but those of 'literary' disincorporation.[19]

I am not sure that the notion of utopia takes this into account. It is a word whose definitional capabilities have been completely devoured by its connotative properties. Sometimes it refers to the mad delusions that lead to totalitarian catastrophe; sometimes it refers, conversely, to the infinite expansion of the field of possibility that resists all forms of totalizing closure. From the point of view that concerns us here, i.e. the point of view of the reconfigurations of the shared sensible order, the word utopia harbours two contradictory meanings. Utopia is, in one respect, the unacceptable, a no-place, the extreme point of a polemical reconfiguration of the sensible, which breaks down the categories that define what is considered to be obvious. However, it is also the configuration of a proper place, a [65] non-polemical distribution of the sensible universe where what one sees, what one says, and what one makes or does are rigorously adapted to one another. Utopias and forms of utopian socialism functioned based on this ambiguity. On the one hand, they dismissed the obvious sensible facts in which the normality of domination is rooted. On the other hand, they proposed a state of affairs where the idea of the community would have its adequate forms of incorporation, a state of affairs that would therefore abolish the dispute concerning the relations of words to things that makes up the heart of politics. In *The Nights of Labor*, I analysed from this perspective the complex encounter between workers and the engineers of utopia. What the Saint-Simonian engineers proposed was a new, real body for the community where the water and rail routes marked out on the ground would take the place of paper dreams and the illusions of speech. The workers, for their part, did not set practice in contrast with utopia; they conferred upon the latter the characteristic of being 'unreal', of being a montage of words and images appropriate for reconfiguring the territory of the visible, the thinkable, and the possible. The 'fictions' of art and politics are therefore heterotopias rather than utopias. [66]

On Art and Work[20]

The link between artistic practice and its apparent outside, i.e. work, is essential to the hypothesis of a 'factory of the sensible'. How do you yourself conceive of such a link (exclusion, distinction, indifference...)? Is it possible to speak of 'human activity' in general and include artistic practices within it, or are these exceptions when compared to other practices?

The first possible meaning of the notion of a 'factory of the sensible' is the formation of a shared sensible world, a common habitat, by the weaving together of a plurality of human activities. However, the idea of a 'distribution of the sensible' implies something more. A 'common' world is never simply an *ethos*, a shared abode, that results from the sedimentation of a certain number of intertwined acts. It is always a polemical distribution of modes of being and 'occupations' in [67] a space of possibilities. It is from this perspective that it is possible to raise the question of the relationship between the 'ordinariness' of work and artistic 'exceptionality'. Here again referencing Plato can help lay down the terms of the problem. In the third book of the *Republic*, the mimetician is no longer condemned simply for the falsity and the pernicious nature of the images he presents, but he is condemned in accordance with a principle of division of labour that was already used to exclude artisans from any shared political space: the mimetician is, by definition, a double being. He does two things at once, whereas the principle of a well-organized community is that each person only does the one thing that they were destined to do by their 'nature'. In one sense, this statement says everything: the idea of work is not initially the idea of a determined activity, a process of material transformation. It is the idea of a distribution of the sensible: an impossibility of doing 'something else' based on an 'absence of time'. This 'impossibility' is part of the incorporated conception of the community. It establishes work as the necessary relegation of the worker to the private space-time of his occupation, his exclusion from participation in what is common to the community.[21] The mimetician brings confusion to [68] this distribution: he is a man of duplication, a worker who does two things at once. Perhaps the correlate to this principle is the most important thing: the mimetician provides a public stage for the 'private' principle of work. He sets up a stage for what is common to the community with what should determine the confinement of each person to his or her place. It is this redistribution of the sensible that constitutes his noxiousness, even more than the danger of simulacra weakening souls. Hence, artistic practice is not the outside of work but its displaced form of visibility. The democratic distribution of the sensible makes the worker into a double being. It removes the artisan from 'his' place, the domestic space of work, and gives him 'time' to occupy the space of public discussions and take on the identity of a deliberative citizen. The mimetic act of splitting in two, which is at work in theatrical space, consecrates this duality and makes it visible. The exclusion of the mimetician, from the Platonic point of view, goes hand in hand with the formation of a community where work is in 'its' place.

The principle of fiction that governs the representative regime of art is a way of stabilizing the artistic exception, of assigning it to a *technē*, which means two things: the art of imitations is a technique and not a lie. It ceases to be [69] a simulacrum, but at the same time it ceases to be the displaced visibility of work, as a distribution of the sensible. The imitator is no longer the double being against whom it is necessary to posit the city where each person only does a single thing. The art of imitations is able to inscribe its specific hierarchies and exclusions in the major distribution of the liberal arts and the mechanical arts.

The aesthetic regime of the arts disrupts this apportionment of spaces. It does not simply call into question mimetic division – i.e. the mimetic act of splitting in two – in favour of an immanence of thought in sensible matter. It also calls into question the neutralized status of *technē*, the idea of technique as the imposition of a form of thought on inert matter. That is to say that it brings to light, once again, the distribution of *occupations* that upholds the apportionment of domains of activity. This theoretical and political operation is at the heart of Schiller's *On the Aesthetic Education of Man*. Behind the Kantian definition of aesthetic judgement as a judgement without concepts – without the submission of the intuitive given to conceptual determination –, Schiller indicates the political distribution that is the matter at stake: the division between those who act and those who are acted upon, between the cultivated classes [70] that have access to a totalization of lived experience and the uncivilized classes immersed in the parcelling out of work and of sensory experience. Schiller's 'aesthetic' state, by suspending the opposition between active understanding and passive sensibility, aims at breaking down – with an idea of art – an idea of society based on the opposition between those who think and decide and those who are doomed to material tasks.

In the nineteenth century, this *suspension* of work's negative value became the assertion of its positive value as the very form of the shared effectivity of thought and community. This mutation occurred via the transformation of the suspension inherent in the 'aesthetic state' into the positive assertion of the aesthetic *will*. Romanticism declared that the becoming-sensible of all thought and the becoming-thought of all sensible materiality was the very goal of the activity of thought in general. In this way, art once again became a symbol of work. It anticipates the end – the elimination of oppositions – that work is not yet in a position to attain by and for itself. However, it does this insofar as it is a *production*, the identification of a process of material execution with a community's self-presentation of its meaning. Production asserts itself [71] as the principle behind a new distribution of the sensible insofar as it unites, in one and the same concept, terms that are traditionally opposed: the activity of manufacturing and visibility. Manufacturing meant inhabiting the private and lowly space-time of labour for sustenance. Producing unites the act of manufacturing with the act of bringing to light, the act of defining a new relationship between *making* and *seeing*. Art anticipates work because it carries out its principle: the transformation of sensible matter into the community's self-presentation. The texts written by the young Marx that confer upon work the status of the generic essence of mankind were only possible on the basis of German Idealism's aesthetic programme, i.e. art as the transformation of thought into the sensory experience of the community. It is this initial programme, moreover, that laid the foundation for the thought and practice of the 'avant-gardes' in the 1920s: abolish art as a separate activity, put it back to work, that is to say, give it back to life and its activity of working out its own proper meaning.

I do not mean by this that the modern valorization of work is only the result of the new way for thinking about art. On the one hand, the *aesthetic* mode of thought is much more than a way of thinking about art. It is an idea of thought, linked to an idea of the distribution [72] of the sensible. On the other hand, it is also necessary to think about the way in which artists' art found itself defined on the basis of a twofold promotion of work: the economic promotion of work as the name for the fundamental human activity, but also the struggles of the proletariat to bring labour out of the night surrounding it, out of its exclusion from shared visibility and speech. It is necessary to abandon the lazy and absurd schema that contrasts the aesthetic cult of art for art's sake with the rising power of industrial labour. Art can show signs of being an exclusive activity insofar as it is work. Better informed than the demystifiers of the twentieth century, the critics in Flaubert's time indicated what links the cult of the sentence to the valorization of work, said to be wordless: the Flaubertian aesthete is a pebble breaker. At the time of the Russian Revolution, art and production would be identified because they came under one and the same principle concerning the redistribution of the sensible, they came under one and the same virtue of action that opens up a form of visibility at the same time as it manufactures objects. The cult of art presupposes a revalorization of the abilities attached to the very idea of work. However, this idea is less the discovery of the essence of human activity than a recomposition of the landscape of the visible, a recomposition of the [73] relationship between doing, making, being, seeing, and saying. Whatever might be the specific type of economic circuits they lie within, artistic practices are not 'exceptions' to other practices. They represent and reconfigure the distribution of these activities.

Interview for the English Edition

The Janus-Face of Politicized Art:[22]
Jacques Rancière in Interview with Gabriel Rockhill

HISTORICAL AND HERMENEUTIC METHODOLOGY

– *I would like to begin with a question concerning methodology. On several occasions, you call into question the symptomatology that attempts to unveil the truth hidden behind the obscure surface of appearances, whether it is Althusser's science, Freud's etiology, or the social sciences in general. In your own research on the distributions of the sensible that underlie historical configurations of art and politics, how do you avoid this logic of the hidden and the apparent? How would you describe your own historical and hermeneutic methodology if 'there is no science [...] but of the hidden'?[23]*

– 'There is no science [...] but of the hidden' is a phrase by Bachelard that had been taken up by the Althusserians. Thus, it was an ironic quotation *against* the vision that presupposes the necessity of finding or constructing the hidden. It was an ironic quotation directed at Althusser's philosophy as well as at Bourdieu's sociology or the history of the *Annales* School. I by no means think, for my part, that there is no science but of the hidden. I always try to think in terms of horizontal distributions, combinations between systems of possibilities, not in terms of surface and substratum. Where one searches for the hidden beneath the apparent, a position of mastery is established. I have tried to conceive of a topography that does not presuppose this position of mastery. It is possible, from any given point, to try to reconstruct the conceptual network that makes it possible to conceive of a statement, that causes a painting or a piece of music to make an impression, that causes reality to appear transformable or inalterable. This is in a way the main theme of my research. I do not mean by that that it is a principle or a starting point. I began, myself as well, from the stereotyped vision of science as a search for the hidden. Then I constructed, little by little, an egalitarian or anarchist theoretical position that does not presuppose this vertical relationship of top to bottom.

– *Does that mean that the regimes of art are not transcendental conditions of possibility for history in the sense of Foucault, but rather conditions of probability that are immanent in history?*

– I try not to think about this in terms of the philosophy of history. As for the term *transcendental*, it is necessary to see what this word can mean. The transcendental is something like a reduction of the transcendent that can either bring the transcendent back into the immanent or, on the contrary, make the immanent take flight once again into the transcendent. I would say that my approach is a bit similar to Foucault's. It retains the principle from the Kantian transcendental that replaces the dogmatism of truth with the search for conditions of possibility. At the same time, these conditions are not conditions for thought in general, but rather conditions immanent in a particular system of thought, a particular system of expression. I differ from Foucault insofar as his archaeology seems to me to follow a schema of historical necessity according to which, beyond a certain chasm, something is no longer thinkable, can no longer be formulated. The visibility of a form of expression as an artistic form depends on a historically constituted regime of perception and intelligibility. This does not mean that it becomes invisible with the emergence of a new regime. I thus try at one and the same to historicize the transcendental and to de-historicize these systems of conditions of possibility. Statements or forms of expression undoubtedly depend on historically constituted systems of possibilities that determine forms of visibility or criteria of evaluation, but this does not mean that we jump from one system to another in such a way that the possibility of the new system coincides with the impossibility of the former system. In this way, the aesthetic regime of art, for example, is a system of possibilities that is historically constituted but that does not abolish the representative regime, which was previously dominant. At a given point in time, several regimes coexist and intermingle in the works themselves.

UNIVERSALITY, HISTORICITY, EQUALITY

— Your claim concerning the universal status of political equality seems to contradict the generalized historicism that characterizes your reflection on aesthetics. However, the 'only universal' is not based on an a priori *foundation, and it is properly speaking a polemical universal that is only actualized in spaces of dispute. Is universality therefore always dependent on a historical implementation? Is it, so to speak, historicized in turn? Or is there a transcendental point that escapes history?*

— There are two questions in your question. First of all, is it a contradiction to emphasize, on the one hand, a political universal and, on the other hand, the historicity of regimes for the identification of art? I do not think so. Both of these approaches refer back to the same rational core, which is the critique of those forms of discourse that in fact play a double game by using general ahistorical concepts of art and politics, while at the same time linking both of them to historical destinies by declaring our epoch to be the age of the 'end' of art or politics. What I intend to show in both cases is that *art* and *politics* are contingent notions. The fact that there are always forms of power does not mean that there is always such a thing as politics, and the fact that there is music or sculpture in a society does not mean that art is constituted as an independent category. From this perspective, I chose two different forms of argumentation. For the former, I showed that politics was not tied to a determined historical project, as it is declared to be by those who identify its end with the end of the project of emancipation begun by the French Revolution. Politics exists when the figure of a specific subject is constituted, a supernumerary subject in relation to the calculated number of groups, places, and functions in a society. This is summed up in the concept of the *dēmos*. Of course, this does not prevent there from being historical forms of politics, and it does not exclude the fact that the forms of political subjectivization that make up modern democracy are of an entirely different complexity than the people in Greek democratic cities.

Concerning art, it seemed necessary to me to emphasize the existence of historical regimes of identification in order to dismiss, at one and the same time, the false obviousness of art's eternal existence and the confused images of artistic 'modernity' in terms of a 'critique of representation'. I evoked the fact that art in the singular has only existed for two centuries and that this existence in the singular meant the upheaval of the coordinates through which the 'fine arts' had been located up to then as well as the disruption of the norms of fabrication and assessment that these coordinates presupposed. I showed that if the properties of each one of these regimes of identification was studied, it was possible to dissipate quite a lot of the haze surrounding the idea of a 'modern project' of art and its completion or failure. This was done, for example, by showing that phenomena considered to be part of a postmodern rupture (such as the mixture of the arts or the combination of mediums) actually fall within the possibilities inherent in the aesthetic regime of art. In both cases, it is a matter of setting a singularized universal against an undetermined universal and contrasting one form of historicizing (in terms of contingent regimes organizing a field of possibilities) with another form of historicizing (in terms of teleology).

The second question concerns the universal and its historicity. My thesis is indeed that the political universal only takes effect in a singularized form. It is distinguished, in this way, from the State universal conceived of as what makes a community out of a multiplicity of individuals. Equality is what I have called a presupposition. It is not, let it be understood, a founding ontological principle but a condition that only functions when it is put into action. Consequently, politics is not based on equality in the sense that others try to base it on some general human predisposition such as language or fear. Equality is actually the condition required for being able to think politics. However, equality is not, to begin with, political in itself. It takes effect in lots of circumstances that have nothing political about them (in the simple fact, for example, that two interlocutors can understand one another). Secondly, equality only generates politics when it is implemented in the specific form of a particular case of dissensus.

– *Is this actualization of equality also to be found in aesthetics, and more specifically in what you call democratic writing? Is it the same universal presupposition that is at work?*

– I do not set down equality as a kind of transcendental governing every sphere of activity, and thus art in particular. That said, art as we know it in the aesthetic regime is the implementation of a certain equality. It is based on the destruction of the hierarchical system of the fine arts. This does not mean, however, that equality in general, political equality, and aesthetic equality are all equivalent. Literature's general condition as a modern form of the art of writing is what I have called, by rerouting the Platonic critique, the democracy of the written word. However, the democracy of the written word is not yet democracy as a political form. And literary equality is not simply the equality of the written word; it is a certain way in which equality can function that can tend to distance it from any form of political equality. To state it very crudely, literature was formed in the nineteenth century by establishing its own proper equality. Flaubert's equality of style is thus at once an implementation of the democracy of the written word and its refutation. Moreover, this equality of style aims at revealing an immanent equality, a passive equality of all things that stands in obvious contrast with the political subjectivization of equality in all its forms.

– *What then are the heuristic advantages of the notion of equality for explaining the major changes between 'classical art' and 'modern art'? Why do you propose the notion of equality for thinking through the specificity of the aesthetic regime of the arts instead of accepting all of the preconceived opinions on the destiny of modern art: the transition from the representative to the non-representative, the realization of the autonomy of the aesthetic sphere, art's intransitive turn, etc.?*

– Once again, I am not proposing equality as a conceptual category for art, but I think that the notion of aesthetic equality allows us to rethink certain incoherent categories integral to what is called artistic 'modernity'. Let's take intransitivity for example. Intransitivity is supposed to mean that writers will henceforth deal with language instead of telling a story, or that painters will distribute fields of colour instead of painting warhorses or naked women (Maurice Denis). However, this supposed dismissal of subject matter first presupposes the establishment of a regime of equality regarding subject matter. This is what 'representation' was in the first place, not resemblance as some appear to believe, but the existence of necessary connections between a type of subject matter and a form of expression. This is how the hierarchy of genres functioned in poetry or painting.[24] 'Intransitive' literature or painting means first of all a form of literature or painting freed from the systems of expression that make a particular sort of language, a particular kind of composition, or possibly a particular type of colour appropriate for the nobility or banality of a specific subject matter. The concept of intransitivity does not allow us to understand this. It is clear that this concept does not work in literature. In a way, literature always says something. It simply says it in modes that are set off from a certain standard idea of a message. Some have attempted to contrast literary intransitivity with communication, but the language of literature can be as transparent as the language of communication. What functions differently is the relationship between saying and meaning. This is where a dividing line becomes visible, which coincides with the implementation of another form of equality, not the equality of communicators but the equality of the communicated. Likewise, for abstract painting to appear, it is first necessary that the subject matter of painting be considered a matter of indifference. This began with the idea that painting a cook with her kitchen utensils was as noble as painting a general on a battlefield. In literature, it began with the idea that it was not necessary to adopt a particular style to write about nobles, bourgeois, peasants, princes, or valets. The equality of subject matter and the indifference regarding modes of expression is prior to the possibility of abandoning all subject matter for abstraction. The former is the condition of the latter.

I am not looking to establish a way of thinking modern art on the basis of equality. I try to show that there are several kinds of equality at play, that literary equality is not the same thing as democratic equality or the universal exchangeability of commodities.

– Regarding the different forms of equality, how do you distinguish writing, criticized by Plato as an orphan letter that freely circulates without knowing who it should address, and the indifferent flow of capital? More specifically, how do you distinguish, in the nineteenth century, between the literary equality that you pinpoint in an author like Flaubert and the equality of exchange?

– The equality of the written word is not the same thing as the equality of exchange. The democracy of the written word does not come down to the arbitrary nature of signs. When Plato criticizes the availability of the written word, he calls into question a form of unsupervised appropriation of language that leads to the corruption of legitimacy. The circulation of the written word destroys the principle of legitimacy that would have the circulation of language be such that it leaves the proper transmitter and goes to the proper receiver by the proper channel. 'Proper' language is guaranteed by a proper distribution of bodies. The written word opens up a space of random appropriation, establishes a principle of untamed difference that is altogether unlike the universal exchangeability of commodities. To put it very crudely, you cannot lay your hands on capital like you can lay your hands on the written word. The play of language without hierarchy that violates an order based on the hierarchy of language is something completely different than the simple fact that a euro is worth a euro and that two commodities that are worth a euro are equivalent to one another. It is a matter of knowing if absolutely anyone can take over and redirect the power invested in language. This presupposes a modification in the relationship between the circulation of language and the social distribution of bodies, which is not at all at play in simple monetary exchange.

An idea of democracy has been constructed according to which democracy would be the simple system of indifference where one vote is equal to another just as a cent is worth a cent, and where the 'equality of conditions' would be equal to monetary equivalence. From this perspective, it is possible to posit literary indifference, Flaubert's indifference of style for example, as analogous to democratic and commercial indifference. However, I think that it is precisely at this point that it is necessary to bring the differences back into play. There is not an analogy but a conflict between forms of equality, which itself functions at several levels in literature. Let's take *Madame Bovary* as an example. On the one hand, the absolutization of style corresponds to a principle of democratic equality. The adultery committed by a farmer's daughter is as interesting as the heroic actions of great men. Moreover, at a time when nearly everyone knows how to read, almost anyone has access, as a result of the egalitarian circulation of writing, to the fictitious life of Emma Bovary and can make it their own. Consequently, there is a veritable harmony between the random circulation of the written word and a certain literary absolute. On the other hand, however, Flaubert constructs his literary equality in opposition to the random circulation of the written word and to the type of 'aesthetic' equality it produces. At the heart of *Madame Bovary* there is a struggle between two forms of equality. In one sense, Emma Bovary is the heroine of a certain aesthetic democracy. She wants to bring art into her life, both into her love life and into the décor of her house. The novel is constructed as a constant polemic against a farm girl's desire to bring art into life. It contrasts 'art in life' (this will later be called the aestheticization of daily life) with a form of art that is in books and only in books.

Nonetheless, neither art in books nor art in life is synonymous with democracy as a form for constructing dissensus over 'the given' of public life. Neither the former nor the latter, moreover, is equivalent to the indifference inherent in the reign of commodities and the reign of money. Flaubert constructs a literary indifference that maintains a distance from any political subjectivization. He asserts a molecular equality of affects that stands in opposition to the molar equality of subjects constructing a democratic political scene. This is summed up in the phrase where he says he is less interested in someone dressed in rags than in the lice that are feeding on him, less interested in social inequality than in molecular equality. He constructs his book as an implementation of the microscopic equality that makes each sentence equal to another – not in length but in intensity – and that makes each sentence, in the end, equal to the entire book. He constructs this equality in opposition to several other kinds of equality: commercial equality, democratic political equality, or equality as a lifestyle such as the equality his heroine tries to put into practice.

POSITIVE CONTRADICTION

– *What is the historical status of the contradiction between incorporation and disincorporation – the struggle between body and spirit – that you find at work in Flaubert as well as in Balzac, Mallarmé, and Proust? Why has this contradiction been a crucial determining factor for modern literature, as well as for egalitarian democracy?*

– Incorporation and disincorporation do not mean body and spirit. In the Christian tradition, body and spirit go together and stand in opposition to the 'dead letter'. Language is incorporated when it is guaranteed by a body or a material state; it is disincorporated when the only materiality that supports it is its own. The conflict between these two states of language is at the heart of literature such as it was developed in the nineteenth century as an aesthetic regime of writing. In one respect, literature means disincorporation. The traditional expressive relationships between words, feelings, and positions collapsed at the same time as the 'social' hierarchies they corresponded to. There were no longer noble words and ignoble words, just as there was no longer noble subject matter and ignoble subject matter. The arrangement of words was no longer guaranteed by an ordered system of appropriateness between words and bodies. There was, on the one hand, a vast egalitarian surface of free words that could ultimately amount to the limitless indifferent chatter of the world. On the other hand, however, there was the desire to replace the old expressive conventions with a direct relationship between the potential of words and the potential of bodies, where language would be the direct expression of a potential for being that was immanent in beings. This is what is at work in Balzac, as I have attempted to show in *La Parole muette* and *The Flesh of Words*. In his work, it is the things themselves that speak. The course of destiny is already written on the façade of a house or on the clothing worn by an individual. An 'everything speaks' (Novalis) is immanent in things, and literature conceives of itself as a revival, an unfurling, a deciphering of this 'everything speaks'. It dreams of constructing a new body for writing on this foundation. This will later become Rimbaud's project in developing an 'Alchemy of the Word' or Mallarmé's dream of a poem choreographing the movements of the Idea, before becoming the Futurist language of new energies or the Surrealist dream of a language of desire that can be read in graffiti, shop signs, or catalogues of out-of-date merchandise.

The nineteenth century was haunted – negatively – by the Platonic paradigm of the democratic dissolution of the social body, by the fanciful correlation between democracy/individualism/Protestantism/ revolution/the disintegration of the social bond. This can be expressed in more or less poetic or scientific terms (sociology as a science was born from this obsession with the lost social bond), more or less reactionary or progressive terms, but the entire century was haunted by the imminent danger that an indifferent equality would come to reign and by the idea that it was necessary to oppose it with a new meaning of the communal body. Literature was a privileged site where this became visible. It was at one and the same time a way of exhibiting the reign of indifferent language and, conversely, a way of remaking bodies with words and even a way of leading words toward their cancellation in material states. I studied this tension in Balzac's *The Village Rector*. The novel is the story of a crime caused by a book that intervenes in the working-class life of a young girl not destined to read it. In contrast with the fatal words written on paper, there is a good form of writing, one that does not circulate but is inscribed in things themselves. However, this form of writing can only mean, in the end, the self-cancellation of literature: the daughter of the people, lost by a book, 'writes her repentance' in the form of canals that will enrich a village. This is the precise equivalent of the Saint-Simonian theory that opposes the paths of communication opened up in the earth to the chatter of democratic newspapers.

This tension is expressed in a completely different manner in the work of Mallarmé or Rimbaud. Mallarmé attempted to identify the poetic function with a symbolic economy that would supplement the simple equality of coins, words in the newspaper, and votes in a ballot box. He opposes the vertical celebration of the community to the horizontality of the 'democratic terreplein' (Plato's arithmetical equality). Rimbaud attempts, for his part, to elaborate a new song for the community, expressed in a new word that would be accessible to all the senses.[25] This is, however, where the contradiction appears. The 'alchemy of the word' that is supposed to construct a new body only has at its disposition a bric-a-brac of various forms of orphaned writing: books in school-taught Latin, silly refrains, small erotic books with spelling errors...

— Are there authors who escape this logic that dominates the nineteenth century? How would you react to the criticism that consists in accusing you of privileging a certain negative dialectic of history, a dialectic without a definitive resolution between incorporation and disincorporation, at the expense of the social dynamic of history or the plurality of literary and artistic practices?

— It all depends on what one calls a 'negative dialectic'. What I have attempted to think through is not a negative dialectic but rather a positive contradiction. Literature has been constructed as a tension between two opposing rationalities: a logic of disincorporation and dissolution, whose result is that words no longer have any guarantee, and a hermeneutic logic that aims at establishing a new body for writing. This tension is, for me, a galvanizing tension, a principle of work and not by any means a principle of 'inertia' or 'non-work'.[26]

Are there authors who escape this tension? Undoubtedly. I have not sought to privilege a particular type of author. I have obviously chosen authors that belong to a homogenous universe – France in the century 'after the Revolution' –, which very forcefully lays down the political stakes of writing. An identical tension is still however to be found in non-French authors from the twentieth century. Take Virginia Woolf, for instance, and you will see that she strives in the same way toward a language that eliminates its contingency, at the risk of brushing shoulders with the language of the mad. Take Joyce, and you will find a vast expanse of stereotypes without end at the same time as the ascent toward language's necessity, which would also be the necessity of myth. Take, for instance, an Italian communist author like Pavese. In his work, there is a paratactic style and a realist language that is faithful to the ways of mediocre and commonplace characters, working-class or middle-class characters without depth. There is a modernism that borders on minimalism. At the same time, there is an entire mythological dimension that, like in Joyce's work, refers back to Vico: a desire to rediscover, within 'modern' triviality, the powers of myth enveloped in language. I am thinking, in particular, of the *Dialogues with Leuco* that he wrote as though in the margin of his 'realist' narratives, as a way of mining beneath their horizontal language. The same kind of tensions are to be found in all of modern literature.

– *Is not this even the case with the Scriptures? You find there to be at least a proximity between Scripture and the contradiction of modern literature.*

– I am not at all a specialist in Scripture. You are undoubtedly alluding to *The Flesh of Words* and to the remarks I made in Auerbach's margins. It is Auerbach who sets the verticality of the evangelical narrative against the horizontality of Homeric description. In the episode of Peter's denial, he stresses the little picturesque indications that convey the drama of a common man taken hold of by the grand mystery. He sees in this the original model of novelistic realism. I oppose this idea by maintaining that these little picturesque indications in fact amount to a writing machine. It is less a matter of conveying the intimate drama of the common man than linking the episodes of the New Testament to the episodes of the Old Testament in order to show that Peter's denial, like the other episodes in the Gospel, had already been foretold in the Old Testament. This means that it is possible to derive two antagonistic models of incarnation itself. According to one model, writing conceals itself in the flesh. According to the other, writing openly reveals itself as the disembodied condition of any glorious flesh. I have attempted to show how it was possible to derive from these models two opposed ideas of novelistic reality and how the two paradigms could become intermingled.

POLITICIZED ART

– Barring a few exceptions, you avoid the concept of commitment. Do you reject this notion because of the false dichotomy it presupposes between art for art's sake and social reality? Are its inadequacies as a concept due to the fact that it is based on simplistic distinctions between the voluntary and the involuntary, between the individual and society?

– It is an in-between notion that is vacuous as an aesthetic notion and also as a political notion. It can be said that an artist is committed as a person, and possibly that he is committed by his writings, his paintings, his films, which contribute to a certain type of political struggle. An artist can be committed, but what does it mean to say that his art is committed? Commitment is not a category of art. This does not mean that art is apolitical. It means that aesthetics has its own politics, or its own meta-politics. That is what I was saying earlier regarding Flaubert and microscopic equality. There are politics of aesthetics, forms of community laid out by the very regime of identification in which we perceive art (hence pure art as well as committed art). Moreover, a 'committed' work of art is always made as a kind of combination between these objective politics that are inscribed in the field of possibility for writing, objective politics that are inscribed as plastic or narrative possibilities.[27] The fact that someone writes to serve a cause or that someone discusses workers or the common people instead of aristocrats, what exactly is this going to change regarding the precise conditions for the elaboration and reception of a work of art? Certain means are going to be chosen instead of others according to a principle of adaptation. The problem, however, is that the adaptation of expression to subject matter is a principle of the representative tradition that the aesthetic regime of art has called into question. That means that there is no criterion for establishing a correspondence between aesthetic virtue and political virtue. There are only choices. A progressive or revolutionary painter or novelist in the 1920s and 1930s will generally choose a chaotic form in order to show that the reigning order is just as much a disorder. Like Dos Passos, he will represent a shattered reality: fragmented stories of erratic individual destinies that translate, by their illogicality, the logic of the capitalist order. Painters like Dix or Grosz in Germany, on the other hand, will represent a human/inhuman universe, a universe where human beings drift between marionettes, masks, and skeletons. They thereby play between two types of inhumanity: the inhumanity of the masks and automatons of the social parade and the inhumanity of the deadly machine that upholds this parade. These plastic or narrative devices can be identified with an exemplary political awareness of the contradictions inherent in a social and economic order. They can, however, just as well be denounced as reactionary nihilism or even considered to be pure formal machines without political content. Novelistic fragmentation or pictorial carnivalization lend themselves just as well to describing the chaos of the capitalist world from the point of view of class struggle as to describing, from a nihilistic point of view, the chaos of a world where class struggle is itself but one element in the Dionysian chaos. Take, for instance, a cinematic equivalent: the American films from the 1970s and 1980s on Vietnam, like Cimino's *The Deer Hunter*, where the war scenes are essentially scenes of Russian roulette. It can be said that the message is the derisory nature of the war. It can just as well be said that the message is the derisory nature of the struggle against the war.

There are no criteria. There are formulas that are equally available whose meaning is often in fact decided upon by a state of conflict that is exterior to them. For example, there is the social narrative in the form of a modern epic that confers a mythological dimension on its characters. *Les Misérables* is the prototype of this kind of narrative. Depending on the times, it has been seen as a catechism with socialist leanings, ignorant bourgeois sentimentalism over class struggle, or a first-rate poem whose democratic meaning is not to be found in the din of the revolutionary barricades but in the individual and quasi-subterranean obstinacy of Jean Valjean. The core of the problem is that there is no criterion for establishing an appropriate correlation between the politics of aesthetics and the aesthetics of politics. This has nothing to do with the claim made by some people that art and politics should not be mixed. They intermix in any case; politics has its aesthetics, and aesthetics has its politics. But there is no formula for an appropriate correlation. It is the state of politics that decides that Dix's paintings in the 1920s, 'populist' films by Renoir, Duvivier, or Carné in the 1930s, or films by Cimino or Scorsese in the 1980s appear to harbour a political critique or appear, on the contrary, to be suited to an apolitical outlook on the irreducible chaos of human affairs or the picturesque poetry of social differences.

– *Does this mean that the act of judging the political import of works of art is always anchored in a precise socio-historical situation? In that case, just as there is no point of view outside history, as you suggested earlier, there is no general formula that establishes a constant link between an artistic form and a political meaning?*

– There are politics of art that are perfectly identifiable. It is thoroughly possible, therefore, to single out the form of politicization at work in a novel, a film, a painting, or an installation. If this politics coincides with an act of constructing political dissensus, this is something that the art in question does not control. Brecht's theatre, the archetypal form of 'politicized' art, is built on an extremely complex and cunning equilibrium between forms of political pedagogy and forms of artistic modernism. He constantly plays between means of coming to political awareness and means of undermining the legitimacy of great art, which found expression in the theatre by admixtures with the 'minor' performing arts: marionette shows, pantomime performances, the circus, the music hall or cabaret, not to mention boxing. His 'epic theatre' is a combination between a pedagogical logic legitimated by the Marxist corpus and, on the other hand, techniques of fragmentation and the mixture of opposites that are specific to the history of theatre and production in the 1910s and 1920s. The political formula is identifiable. Nevertheless – between Brecht's exile in Denmark or the United States, the official position in the German Democratic Republic, and his adoption by the European intellectual elites in the 1950s – the encounter between this particular form of politics and its supposed audience (workers conscious of the capitalist system) never took place, which means that its suitability to its militant referent was never really tested.

– *What is the role played by what you call 'heterology' in politicized art? I am thinking in particular of one of your analyses of Rossellini's* Europa '51 *where you establish a connection between the main character's encounter with the uncanny – the moment when Irene leaves the framework of her immediate surroundings in order to go and look elsewhere, thereby confounding the established aesthetico-political categories – and the actualization of equality?*[28]

– This means that an aesthetic politics always defines itself by a certain recasting of the distribution of the sensible, a reconfiguration of the given perceptual forms. The notion of 'heterology' refers to the way in which the meaningful fabric of the sensible is disturbed: a spectacle does not fit within the sensible framework defined by a network of meanings, an expression does not find its place in the system of visible coordinates where it appears. The dream of a suitable political work of art is in fact the dream of disrupting the relationship between the visible, the sayable, and the thinkable without having to use the terms of a message as a vehicle. It is the dream of an art that would transmit meanings in the form of a rupture with the very logic of meaningful situations. As a matter of fact, political art cannot work in the simple form of a meaningful spectacle that would lead to an 'awareness' of the state of the world. Suitable political art would ensure, at one and the same time, the production of a double effect: the readability of a political signification and a sensible or perceptual shock caused, conversely, by the uncanny, by that which resists signification. In fact, this ideal effect is always the object of a negotiation between opposites, between the readability of the message that threatens to destroy the sensible form of art and the radical uncanniness that threatens to destroy all political meaning.

Europa '51 is, in point of fact, built on a series of ruptures, of displacements out of frame (in the strongest sense of the word and not the technical sense). The first sensible or perceptual world of the bourgeois housewife, for whom the workers are those unknown people who go on strike and disturb urban traffic and transportation, is challenged by a second world: the visit organized by her communist cousin to the cheap apartment buildings where the workers live. However, this structured working-class world where the setting and its meaning coincide is in turn challenged in favour of an open world without coordinates, a world of vague stretches of land, shanty towns, and sub-proletarian wandering, where nothing coincides any longer. The outcome is that the heroine finds herself more and more diverted from any system of correspondences between meanings and the visible. Her own specific question (what words her son, who threw himself down the stairwell, said or would have said) coincides with the discovery of a world progressively loosing its structure where the only answer is charity, according to her, and insanity, according to the representatives of society.

A system of heterologies is indeed put into play here. Furthermore, I had emphasized the way in which this system throws off the pre-constituted political modes of framing. That said, it is clear that refusing to frame the situation in accordance with the communist schema also authorizes framing it according to the Christian schema, which actually has the advantage of framing without walls: the heroine's wandering that I had previously identified with Socratic atopia is, after all, a wandering oriented toward the grace of Spirit, which like the wind 'blows where it wills' (even if it is Rossellini who is playing a bit the role of God the Father).[29]

This means that the play of heterologies always has an undecidable aspect to it. It undoes the sensible fabric – a given order of relations between meanings and the visible – and establishes other networks of the sensible, which can possibly corroborate the action undertaken by political subjects to reconfigure what are given to be facts. There are aesthetic formulas and transformations of these formulas that always define a certain 'politics'. There is not, however, a rule establishing a concordance, nor are there criteria for distinguishing good political films from bad political films. In fact, we should avoid asking the question in terms of criteria for the political evaluation of works of art. The politics of works of art plays itself out to a larger extent – in a global and diffuse manner – in the reconfiguration of worlds of experience based on which police consensus or political dissensus are defined. It plays itself out in the way in which modes of narration or new forms of visibility established by artistic practices enter into politics' own field of aesthetic possibilities. It is necessary to reverse the way in which the problem is generally formulated. It is up to the various forms of politics to appropriate, for their own proper use, the modes of presentation or the means of establishing explanatory sequences produced by artistic practices rather than the other way around.

It is in this sense that I said, at the end of *The Names of History*, that for thinking and writing democratic history, it is necessary to look toward Virginia Woolf more so than toward Émile Zola. This does not mean that Virginia Woolf wrote good social novels. It means that her way of working on the contraction or distension of temporalities, on their contemporaneousness or their distance, or her way of situating events at a much more minute level, all of this establishes a grid that makes it possible to think through the forms of political dissensuality more effectively than the 'social epic's' various forms. There is a limit at which the forms of novelistic micrology establish a mode of individuation that comes to challenge political subjectivization. There is also, however, an entire field of play where their modes of individuation and their means of linking sequences contribute to liberating political possibilities by undoing the formatting of reality produced by state-controlled media, by undoing the relations between the visible, the sayable, and the thinkable.

– Is this what you try to do yourself in your writings on the history of art and politics?

– I do indeed attempt to privilege ways of writing history, presenting situations and arranging statements, ways of constructing relations between cause and effect or between antecedent and consequent that confound the traditional landmarks, the means of presenting objects, inducing meanings and causal schemata, that construct the standard intelligibility of history. I think that a theoretical discourse is always simultaneously an aesthetic form, a sensible reconfiguration of the facts it is arguing about. Claiming that any theoretical statement has a poetic nature is equivalent to breaking down the borders and hierarchies between levels of discourse. Here we have come back to our starting point.

Afterword by Slavoj Žižek

The Lesson of Rancière

F.W.J. Schelling's statement, 'The beginning is the negation of that which begins with it', perfectly fits the itinerary of Jacques Rancière who first appeared on the philosophical scene in the early 1960s as a young Althusserian, one of the contributors (together with Étienne Balibar, Roger Establet and Pierre Macherey) to the path-breaking collective volume *Lire le Capital* from 1965, which, with Althusser's *Pour Marx*, defined the field of 'structuralist Marxism'. However, one did not have to wait long for Rancière's unique voice to explode in a thunder which rocked the Althusserian scene: in 1974, he published *La Leçon d'Althusser* (*The Lesson of Althusser*), a ferocious critical examination of Althusserian structuralist Marxism with its rigid distinction between scientific theory and ideology and its distrust towards any form of spontaneous popular movement which was immediately decried as a form of bourgeois humanism. Against this theoreticist elitism, this insistence on the gap which forever separates the universe of scientific cognition from that of ideological (mis)recognition in which the common masses are immersed, against this stance, which allows theoreticians to 'speak for' the masses, to know the truth about them, Rancière endeavours again and again to elaborate the contours of those magic, violently poetic moments of political subjectivization in which the excluded ('lower classes') put forward their claim to speak for themselves, to effectuate a change in the global perception of social space, so that their claims would have a legitimate place in it.

How, for Rancière, did politics proper begin? With the emergence of the *dēmos* as an active agent within the Greek *polis*, with the emergence of a group which, although without any fixed place in the social edifice (or, at best, occupying a subordinate place), demanded to be included in the public sphere, to be heard on equal footing with the ruling oligarchy or aristocracy, i.e. recognized as a partner in political dialogue and the exercise of power. As Rancière emphasizes against Habermas, political struggle proper is therefore not a rational debate between multiple interests, but, simultaneously, the struggle for one's voice to be heard and recognized as the voice of a legitimate partner: when the 'excluded', from the Greek *dēmos* to Polish workers, protested against the ruling elite (the aristocracy or the *nomenklatura*), the true stakes were not only their explicit demands (for higher wages, work conditions, etc.), but their very right to be heard and recognized as an equal partner in the debate (in Poland, the *nomenklatura* lost the moment it had to accept Solidarity as an equal partner). Furthermore, in protesting the wrong (*le tort*) they suffered, they also presented themselves as the immediate embodiment of society as such, as the stand-in for the Whole of Society in its universality, against the particular power-interests of the aristocracy or oligarchy ('we – the "nothing", not counted in the order – are the people, we are All against others who stand only for their particular privileged interests').

Politics proper thus always involves a kind of short-circuit between the Universal and the Particular: the paradox of a singular which appears as a stand-in for the Universal, destabilizing the 'natural' functional order of relations in the social body. The political conflict resides in the tension between the structured social body where each part has its place – what Rancière calls politics as police in the most elementary sense of maintaining social order – and 'the part with no part' which unsettles this order on account of the empty principle of universality, of what Étienne Balibar calls *égaliberté*, the principled equality-in-freedom of all men qua speaking beings. This identification of the non-part with the Whole, of the part of society with no properly defined place within it (or resisting the allocated subordinate place within it) with the Universal, is the elementary gesture of politicization, discernible in all great democratic events, from the French Revolution (in which *le troisième état* proclaimed itself identical to the Nation as such against the aristocracy and the clergy) to the demise of ex-European Socialism (in which the dissident Forum proclaimed itself representative of the entire society against the Party *nomenklatura*). In this precise sense, politics and democracy are synonymous: the basic aim of antidemocratic politics always – and by definition – is and was depoliticization, i.e. the unconditional demand that 'things should return to normal', with each individual doing his or her particular job. Rancière, of course, emphasizes how the line of separation between the police and politics proper is always blurred and contested; say, in the Marxist tradition, 'proletariat' can be read as the subjectivization of the 'part of no part' elevating its injustice to the ultimate test of universality, and, simultaneously, as the operator which will bring about the establishment of a post-political rational society. Our European tradition contains a series of disavowals of this political moment, of the proper logic of political conflict; Rancière developed them in *La Mésentente* (1995), the masterpiece of his political thought:

- archi-politics: the 'communitarian' attempts to define a traditional close, organically structured homogeneous social space which allows for no void in which the political moment-event can emerge;
- para-politics: the attempt to depoliticize politics (to translate it into the police-logic): one accepts the political conflict, but reformulates it into a competition, within the representational space, between acknowledged parties/agents, for the (temporary) occupation of the place of executive power. Habermasian or Rawlsian ethics are perhaps the last philosophical vestiges of this attitude: the attempt to de-antagonize politics by way of formulating the clear rules to be obeyed so that the agonic procedure of litigation does not explode into politics proper;
- Marxist (or Utopian Socialist) meta-politics: the political conflict is fully asserted, as a shadow-theatre in which processes – whose proper place is on Another Scene (the scene of economic infrastructure) – are played out; the ultimate goal of 'true' politics is thus its self-cancellation, the transformation of the 'administration of people' into the 'administration of things' within a fully self-transparent rational order of collective Will;
- and, one is tempted to supplement Rancière, the most cunning and radical version of this disavowal is ultra-politics, the attempt to depoliticize conflict by way of bringing it to an extreme via the direct militarization of politics: the 'foreclosed' political returns in the real, in the guise of the attempt to resolve the deadlock of political conflict, of *mésentente*, by its false radicalization, i.e. by way of reformulating it as a war between 'Us' and 'Them', our Enemy, where there is no common ground for symbolic conflict.

What we have in all four cases – archi-, para-, meta- and ultra-politics – is thus an attempt to gentrify the properly traumatic dimension of the political: something emerged in ancient Greece under the name of *polis* demanding its rights, and, from the very beginning (i.e. from Plato's *Republic*) to the recent revival of liberal political thought, 'political philosophy' has been an attempt to suspend the destabilizing potential of the political, to disavow and/or regulate it in one way or another: bringing about a return to a pre-political social body, fixing the rules of political competition, etc. 'Political philosophy' is thus, in all its different shapes, a kind of 'defence-formation', and, perhaps, its typology could be established via reference to the different modalities of defence against some traumatic experience in psychoanalysis. In contrast to these four versions, today's 'postmodern' post-politics opens up a new field which involves a stronger negation of politics: it no longer merely 'represses' it, trying to contain it and to pacify the 'returns of the repressed', but much more effectively 'forecloses' it, so that the postmodern forms of ethnic violence, with their 'irrational' excessive character, are no longer simple 'returns of the repressed', but rather present the case of the foreclosed (from the Symbolic) which, as we know from Lacan, returns in the Real.

In post-politics, the conflict of global ideological visions embodied in different parties who compete for power is replaced by a collaboration of enlightened technocrats (economists, public opinion specialists…) and liberal multiculturalists; via the process of negotiation of interests, a compromise is reached in the guise of a more or less universal consensus. The political (the space of litigation in which the excluded can protest the wrong/injustice done to them), foreclosed from the symbolic then returns in the real, in the form of racism. It is crucial to perceive how 'postmodern racism' emerges as the ultimate consequence of the post-political suspension of the political in the reduction of the state to a mere police agent servicing the (consensually established) needs of the market forces and multiculturalist tolerant humanitarianism: the 'foreigner', whose status is never properly regulated, is the indivisible remainder of the transformation of democratic political struggle into the post-political procedure of negotiation and multiculturalist policing. Instead of the political subject 'working class' demanding its universal rights, we get, on the one hand, the multiplicity of particular social strata or groups, each with its problems (the dwindling need for manual workers, etc.), and, on the other hand, the immigrant, more and more prevented from politicizing his predicament of exclusion.

Rancière is right to emphasize how it is against this background that one should interpret the fascination of 'public opinion' with the unique event of the Holocaust: the reference to the Holocaust as the ultimate, unthinkable, apolitical crime, as the Evil so radical that it cannot be politicized (accounted for by a political dynamic), serves as the operator which allows us to depoliticize the social sphere, to warn against the presumption of politicization. The Holocaust is the name for the unthinkable apolitical excess of politics itself: it compels us to subordinate politics to some more fundamental ethics. The Otherness excluded from the consensual domain of tolerant/rational post-political negotiation and administration returns in the guise of inexplicable pure Evil. What defines postmodern 'post-politics' is thus the secret solidarity between its two opposed Janus faces: on the one hand, the replacement of politics proper by depoliticized 'humanitarian' operations, on the other hand, the violent outbursts of depoliticized 'pure Evil' in the guise of 'excessive' ethnic or religious fundamentalist violence. In short, what Rancière proposes here is a new version of the old Hegelian motto 'Evil resides in the gaze itself which perceives the object as Evil': the contemporary figure of Evil, too 'strong' to be accessible to political analysis (the Holocaust, etc.), appears as such only to the gaze which constitutes it as such (as depoliticized).

In Rancière's diagnosis, today's hegemonic tendency towards post-politics thus compels us to reassert the political in its key dimension; in this, he belongs to the field one is tempted to define as 'post-Althusserian': authors like Balibar, Alain Badiou, up to Ernesto Laclau, whose starting position was close to Althusser. The first thing to note here is how they are all opposed to the most elaborated 'formal' theory of democracy in contemporary French thought, that of Claude Lefort. In an explicit reference to Lacanian theory, Lefort conceptualized the democratic space as sustained by the gap between the Real and the Symbolic: in a democracy, *the place of Power is structurally empty*, nobody has the 'natural' right to occupy it, those who exert power can do so only temporarily and should not ever coalesce with its place. The elegance of this theory is that, in the same way that Kant rejected the opposition between the traditional ethics of a transcendent substantial Good and the utilitarian grounding of ethics in the individual's contingent empirical interests by way of proposing a purely formal notion of ethical duty, Lefort overcomes the opposition between the Rousseauian 'substantialist' notion of democracy as expressing *la volonté générale* and the liberal notion of democracy as the space of negotiated settlement between the plurality of individual interests, by way of proposing a purely 'formal' notion of democracy. So while Lefort proposes a Kantian transcendental notion of political democracy, the 'post-Althusserians' insist that, within the multitude of real political agents, there is a privileged One, the 'supernumerary' which occupies the place of the 'symptomal torsion' of the whole and thus allows us access to its truth – the pure universal form is linked by a kind of umbilical cord to a 'pathological' element which does not fit into the social Whole.

However, even within this 'post-Althusserian' field, there are considerable differences. While Rancière remains faithful to the populist-democratic impulse, Alain Badiou (whose notion of the 'supernumerary' as the site of the political is very close to Rancière's notion of the 'part with no part') opts for a more 'Platonic' form of politics grounded in the universal form-of-thought. While all democratic Leftists venerate Rosa Luxembourg's famous 'Freedom is freedom for those who think differently', Badiou provokes us to shift the accent from 'differently' to 'think': 'Freedom is freedom for those who think differently' – ONLY for those who REALLY THINK, even if differently, not for those who just blindly (unthinkingly) act out their opinions... In his famous short poem 'The Solution' from 1953 (published in 1956), Brecht mocks the arrogance of the Communist *nomenklatura* when faced with the workers' revolt: 'Would it not be easier for the government to dissolve the people and elect another?' However, this poem is not only politically opportunistic, the obverse of his letter of solidarity with the East German Communist regime published in *Neues Deutschland* – to put it brutally, Brecht wanted to cover both his flanks, to profess his support for the regime as well as to hint at his solidarity with the workers, so that whoever won, he would be on the winning side –, but also simply *wrong* in the theoreticopolitical sense: one should bravely admit that it effectively IS a duty – THE duty even – of a revolutionary party to 'dissolve the people and elect another', i.e. to bring about the transubstantiation of the 'old' opportunistic people (the inert 'crowd') into a revolutionary body aware of its historical task. Far from being an easy task, to 'dissolve the people and elect another' is the most difficult of all...

In spite of these differences, there is a feature that unites all the post-Althusserian partisans of 'pure politics': what they oppose to today's post-politics is more Jacobin than Marxist, i.e. it shares with its great opponent, Anglo-Saxon Cultural Studies and their focus on the struggles for recognition, the degradation of the sphere of economy. That is to say, what all the new French (or French oriented) theories of the Political, from Balibar through Rancière and Badiou to Laclau and Mouffe, aim at is – to put it in traditional philosophical terms – the reduction of the sphere of economy (of material production) to an 'ontic' sphere deprived of 'ontological' dignity. Within this horizon, there is simply no place for the Marxian 'critique of political economy': the structure of the universe of commodities and capital in Marx's *Capital* is NOT just that of a limited empirical sphere, but a kind of socio-transcendental *a priori*, the matrix which generates the totality of social and political relations.

The relationship between economy and politics is ultimately that of the well-known visual paradox of the 'two faces or a vase': one either sees the two faces or a vase, never both of them – one has to make a choice. In the same way, one either focuses on the political, and the domain of economy is reduced to the empirical 'servicing of goods', or one focuses on economy, and politics is reduced to a theatre of appearances, to a passing phenomenon which will disappear with the arrival of the developed Communist (or technocratic) society, in which, as Engels already put it, the 'administration of people' will vanish in the 'administration of things'. The 'political' critique of Marxism (the claim that, when one reduces politics to a 'formal' expression of some underlying 'objective' socio-economic process, one loses the openness and contingency constitutive of the political field proper) should thus be supplemented by its obverse: the field of economy is IN ITS VERY FORM irreducible to politics – this level of the FORM of economy (of economy as the determining FORM of the social) is what French 'political post-Marxists' miss when they reduce economy to one of the positive social spheres.

In spite of this critical point, Rancière's theory provides the clearest articulation of the motto which appeared at the demonstrations of the French jobless movement in the mid-90s: *we're not a surplus, we're a plus*. Those who, in the eyes of the administrative power, are perceived as 'a surplus' (laid off, redundant, reduced to silence in a society that subtracted the jobless from the public accounts, that made them into a kind of residue – invisible, inconceivable except as a statistic under a negative sign), should impose themselves as the embodiment of society as such – how? It is here that we encounter the second great breakthrough of Rancière articulated in *Le Partage du sensible*: the *aestheticization of politics*, the assertion of the aesthetic dimension as INHERENT in any radical emancipatory politics. This choice, although grounded in the long French tradition of radical political spectacle, goes against the grain of the predominant notion which sees the main root of Fascism in the elevation of the social body into an aesthetic-organic Whole.

It is not only that, apart from being a political theorist, Rancière wrote a series of outstanding texts on art, especially on cinema – the shift from the political to the aesthetic is inherent in the political itself. The aesthetic metaphor in which a particular element stands for the Universal, is enacted in the properly political short-circuit in which a particular demand stands for the universal gesture of rejecting the power that be. Say, when people strike against a particular measure (new tax regulation, etc.), the true aim of the strike is never just this particular measure – which is why, if those in power give way too fast and repeal this measure, people feel frustrated, since, although their demand was met, they were deprived of what they were really aiming at. And what about the ideological struggle in which a universal conceptual position is always 'schematized' in the Kantian sense of the term, translated into a specific impressive set of images? Recall how, a decade ago, in the UK, the figure of the unemployed single mother was elevated by the conservative media into the cause of all social evils: there is a budget deficit because too much money is spent on supporting single mothers; there is juvenile delinquency because single mothers do not properly educate their offspring... Or recall how the anti-abortion campaigns as a rule put forward the image of a rich career woman neglecting her maternal mission – in blatant contrast to the fact that many more abortions are performed on working-class women who already have many children. These poetic displacements and condensations are not just secondary illustrations of an underlying ideological struggle, but the very terrain of this struggle. If what Rancière refers to as the police-aspect of the political, the rational administration and control of social processes, focuses on the clear categorization of every individual, of every 'visible' social unit, then disturbing such orders of the visible and proposing different lateral links of the visible, unexpected short-circuits, etc., is the elementary form of resistance.

On a more general level, the lesson of Rancière is that one should be careful not to succumb to the liberal temptation of condemning all collective artistic performances as inherently 'totalitarian'. Both the Thingspiel in the early Nazi years and Bertolt Brecht's 'learning plays / *Lehrstueckel*' involved a mass ideologico-aesthetic experience (of songs, speeches and acts) in which spectators themselves served as actors – does this mean that the Left in the 30s participated in the same 'proto-Fascist' totalitarian experience of the 'regressive' immersion into pre-individual community as Nazism (the thesis of, among others, Siegfried Kracauer)? If not, does the difference reside in the fact that the Nazi Thingspiel staged a pathetic-emotional immersion, while Brecht aimed at a distanced, self-observing, reflected process of learning? However, is this standard Brechtian opposition of emotional immersion and reflexive distance sufficient? Let us recall the staged performance of 'Storming the Winter Palace' in Petrograd, on the third anniversary of the October Revolution, on the 7th of November, 1920. Tens of thousands of workers, soldiers, students, and artists worked round the clock, living on kasha (the tasteless wheat porridge), tea, and frozen apples, and preparing the performance at the very place where the event 'really took place' three years earlier; their work was coordinated by the Army officers, as well as by the avant-garde artists, musicians, and directors, from Malevich to Meyerhold. Although this was acting and not 'reality', the soldiers and sailors were playing themselves – many of them not only actually participated in the events of 1917, but were also simultaneously involved in the real battles of the Civil War that were raging in the near vicinity of Petrograd, a city under siege and suffering from severe food shortages. A contemporary commented on the performance: 'The future historian will record how, throughout one of the bloodiest and most brutal revolutions, all of Russia was acting'; and the formalist theoretician Viktor Shklovski noted that 'some kind of elemental process is taking place where the living fabric of life is being transformed into the theatrical'.

Another popular topic of this kind of analysis is the allegedly 'proto-Fascist' character of the mass choreography displaying disciplined movements of thousands of bodies (parades, mass performances in stadiums, etc.); if one also finds this in Socialism, one immediately draws the conclusion about a 'deeper solidarity' between the two 'totalitarianisms'. Such a procedure, the very prototype of ideological liberalism, misses the point: not only are such mass performances not inherently Fascist; they are not even 'neutral', waiting to be appropriated by Left or Right – it was Nazism that stole them and appropriated them from the workers' movement, their original site of birth. None of the 'proto-Fascist' elements is *per se* Fascist, what makes them 'Fascist' is only their specific articulation – or, to put it in Stephen Jay Gould's terms, all these elements are 'ex-apted' by Fascism. In other words, there is no 'Fascism *avant la lettre*', because *it is the letter itself (the nomination) which makes out of the bundle of elements Fascism proper.*

Along the same lines, one should radically reject the notion that discipline (from self-control to bodily training) is a 'proto-Fascist' feature – the very predicate 'proto-Fascist' should be abandoned: it is the exemplary case of a pseudo-concept whose function is to block conceptual analysis. When we say that the organized spectacle of thousands of bodies (or, say, the admiration of sports which demand high effort and self-control like mountain climbing) is 'proto-Fascist', we say strictly nothing, we just express a vague association which masks our ignorance. So when, three decades ago, Kung Fu films were popular (Bruce Lee, etc.), was it not obvious that we were dealing with a genuine working class ideology of youngsters whose only means of success was the disciplinary training of their only possession, their bodies? Spontaneity and the 'let it go' attitude of indulging in excessive freedoms belong to those who have the means to afford it – those who have nothing have only their discipline. The 'bad' bodily discipline, if there is one, is not collective training, but, rather, jogging and body-building as part of the New Age myth of the realization of the Self's inner potentials – no wonder that the obsession with one's body is an almost obligatory part of the passage of ex-Leftist radicals into the 'maturity' of pragmatic politics: from Jane Fonda to Joschka Fischer, the 'period of latency' between the two phases was marked by the focus on one's own body.

It is often claimed that, in his passionate advocacy of the aesthetic dimension as inherent in the political, Rancière nostalgically longs for the nineteenth-century populist rebellions whose era is definitely gone – however, is it really? Is not precisely the 'postmodern' politics of resistance permeated with aesthetic phenomena, from body-piercing and cross-dressing to public spectacles? Does not the curious phenomenon of 'flash mobs' stand for the aesthetico-political protest at its purest, reduced to its minimal frame? People show up at an assigned place at a certain time, perform some brief (and usually trivial or ridiculous) acts, and then disperse again – no wonder flash mobs are described as being urban poetry with no real purpose. Not to mention, of course, cyberspace which abounds with possibilities of playing with multiple (dis)identifications and lateral connections subverting the established social networks... So, far from standing for a nostalgic attachment to a populist past lost by our entry into the global post-industrial society, Rancière's thought is today more actual than ever: in our time of the disorientation of the Left, his writings offer one of the few consistent conceptualizations of *how we are to continue to resist.*

Appendix I

Glossary of Technical Terms

Nota bene

The following definitions aim less at establishing a systematic lexicon for Rancière's work than at providing pragmatic indications to help orient the reader in a unique conceptual and terminological framework. For this reason, each definition is accompanied by references to key passages in Rancière's corpus in order to encourage the reader to resituate these technical terms in the precise theoretical networks that endow them with specific meanings.

Since the majority of the terms defined are specific to Rancière's most recent publications, most of the references are to the body of work he has produced since approximately 1990. However, some references are made to important conceptual developments in Rancière's work that do not use the exact same technical vocabulary. A marked privilege was given to texts available in English, although references to certain key publications in French were indispensable. Complete bibliographical information will be found in Appendix 2. – Trans.

Abbreviations

AT	'The archaeomodern turn'
BP	*Aux Bords du politique* (1998 edition)
CM	*La Chair des mots*
CO	'The cause of the other'
D	*Disagreement: Politics and Philosophy*
DA	'Is there a Deleuzian aesthetics?'
DI	*Le Destin des images*
DME	'Democracy means equality'
DW	'Dissenting words'
FC	*La Fable cinématographique*

HAS	'History and the art system'
IE	*L'Inconscient esthétique*
IS	*The Ignorant Schoolmaster*
LA	*La Leçon d'Althusser*
LPA	'Literature, politics, aesthetics'
M	*Mallarmé: La Politique de la sirène*
ML	'Le malentendu littéraire'
NH	*The Names of History*
PA	*The Politics of aesthetics*
PaA	'Politics and aesthetics'
PhP	*The Philosopher and His Poor*
PIS	'Politics, identification, and subjectivization'
PM	*La Parole muette*
S	'Le 11 septembre et après'
SP	*On the Shores of Politics*
TTP	'Ten theses on politics'
WA	'What aesthetics can mean'

Aesthetic Regime of Art (*Le Régime esthétique de l'art*)
Although traces of this regime are already to be found in such authors as Vico and Cervantes, it has only come to play a dominant role in the last two centuries. The aesthetic regime abolishes the hierarchical **distribution of the sensible** characteristic of the **representative regime of art**, including the privilege of speech over visibility as well as the hierarchy of the arts, their subject matter, and their genres. By promoting the **equality** of represented subjects, the indifference of style with regard to content, and the immanence of meaning in things themselves, the aesthetic regime destroys the system of genres and isolates 'art' in the singular, which it identifies with the paradoxical unity of opposites: *logos* and pathos. However, the singularity of art enters into an interminable contradiction due to the fact that the aesthetic regime also calls into question the very distinction between art and other activities. Strictly speaking, the egalitarian regime of the sensible can only isolate art's specificity at the expense of losing it.
DI 21, 88, 120–1, 125–53; FC 14–18; HAS; IE 25–32; LPA; PA 22–9, 43–4; PM 17–30, 43–52, 86–9; WA.

Aesthetic Revolution (*La Révolution esthétique*)

By calling into question the **representative regime of art** in the name of the **aesthetic regime** around the beginning of the nineteenth century, this 'silent revolution' transformed an organized set of relationships between the visible and the invisible, the perceptible and the imperceptible, knowledge and action, activity and passivity. The aesthetic revolution in the sensible order did not, however, lead to the death of the **representative regime**. On the contrary, it introduced an irresolvable contradiction between diverse elements of the **representative** and **aesthetic regimes of art**.

DI 84–5, 118–22, 135; HAS; IE 25–33; LPA; PA 26–8, 36–7; PaA 205–6; PM 5–30.

Aesthetic Unconscious (*L'Inconscient esthétique*)

Coextensive with the **aesthetic regime of art**, the aesthetic unconscious is paradoxically polarized between the two extremes that characterize **silent speech**. On the one hand, meaning is inscribed like hieroglyphics on the body of things and waits to be deciphered. On the other hand, an unfathomable silence that no voice can adequately render acts as an insurmountable obstacle to signification and meaning. This contradictory conjunction between speech and silence, *logos* and pathos, is not equivalent to the Freudian unconscious or other later interpretations. It is, in fact, the historical terrain upon which competing conceptions of the unconscious have emerged.

IE 41–2, 70–1, 76–7; LPA 20.

Aesthetics (*L'Esthétique*)

In its restricted sense, aesthetics refers neither to art theory in general nor to the discipline that takes art as its object of study. Aesthetics is properly speaking a specific regime for identifying and thinking the arts that Rancière names the **aesthetic regime of art**. In its broad sense, however, aesthetics refers to the **distribution of the sensible** that determines a mode of articulation between forms of action, production, perception, and thought. This general definition extends aesthetics beyond the strict realm of art to include the conceptual coordinates and modes of visibility operative in the political domain.

D 57–9; DA; IE 12–14; LPA 9–12; M 53; PA 10, 13; WA.

Archi-Politics (*L'Archi-politique*)

The prototype of archi-politics, one of the three major types of **political philosophy**, is to be found in Plato's attempt to establish a community based on the integral manifestation of its *logos* in material form. The activities of individual citizens are regulated in relation to their role in the organization of the communal body in such a way that everyone has a designated place and an assigned role. The democratic configuration of **politics** is thereby replaced by the **police order** of a living *nomos* that saturates the entire community and precludes any breaks in the social edifice.

D 61–93; DW; PhP; TTP.

Community of Equals (*La Communauté des égaux*)

A community of equals is not a goal to be attained but rather a presupposition that is in constant need of verification, a presupposition that can never in fact lead to the establishment of an egalitarian social formation since the logic of inequality is inherent in the social bond. A community of equals is therefore a precarious community that implements **equality** in intermittent acts of **emancipation**.

HAS; IS 71–3; SP 63–92.

Consensus (*Le Consensus*)

Prior to being a platform for rational debate, consensus is a specific regime of the sensible, a particular way of positing rights as a community's *archē*. More specifically, consensus is the presupposition according to which every part of a population, along with all of its specific problems, can be incorporated into a political order and taken into account. By abolishing **dissensus** and placing a ban on political **subjectivization**, consensus reduces **politics** to the **police**.

BP 137–8; D 95–140; DW 117–26; S; TTP.

Democracy (*La Démocratie*)

Neither a form of government nor a style of social life, democracy is properly speaking an act of political **subjectivization** that disturbs the **police order** by polemically calling into question the aesthetic coordinates of perception, thought, and action. Democracy is thus falsely identified when it is associated with the consensual self-regulation of the multitude or with the reign of a sovereign collectivity based on subordinating the particular to the universal. It is, in fact, less a state of being than an act of contention that implements various forms of **dissensus**. It can be said to exist only when those who have no title to power, the *dēmos*, intervene as the dividing force that disrupts the *ochlos*. If a community can be referred to as democratic, it is only insofar as it is a 'community of sharing' (*communauté du partage*) in which membership in a common world – not to be confused with a communitarian social formation – is expressed in adversarial terms and coalition only occurs in conflict.

BP 7–15; CM 126–7; D 61–5, 95–121; DME; DW 123–6; LPA; ML; NH 88–103; PA 14–15, 53–8; PM 81–9; SP 20–3, 31–6, 39–107; TTP.

Dēmos (*Le Dēmos*)

Rancière uses this Greek term – meaning 'the commons', 'plebeians', or 'citizens' – interchangeably with 'the **people**' to refer to those who have no share in the communal **distribution of the sensible**. The *dēmos* is thus simultaneously the name of a community and the title signifying the division of a community due to a **wrong**. It is the unique power of assembling and dividing that exceeds all of the arrangements made by legislators; it is the force of communal division that contravenes the **ochlos**' obsession with unification.

CM 126–7; D 61–2; DME 31–2; DW 123–6; PIS; SP 31–6; TTP.

Disagreement (*La Mésentente*)

Prior to linguistic or cultural misunderstanding, Rancière isolates a fundamental discord that results from conflicts over the **distribution of the sensible**. Whereas *la méconnaissance* (lack of comprehension) and *le malentendu* (misunderstanding) produce obstacles to litigation that are – at least in theory – surmountable, *la mésentente* is a conflict over what is meant by 'to speak' and 'to understand' as well as over the horizons of perception that distinguish the audible from the inaudible, the comprehensible from the incomprehensible, the visible from the invisible. A case of disagreement arises when the perennial persistence of a **wrong** enters into conflict with the established **police order** and resists the forms of juridical litigation that are imposed on it.

D vii–xiii, 43–60; DME 35; DW 113–16; ML.

Dispute (*Le Litige*)
A *political* dispute concerns the very existence of **politics** as distinct from the **police**. Unlike *juridical* disputes, which take place within the **police order**, *le litige politique* brings **politics** proper into existence by introducing a veritable **dissensus** that splits in two the shared world of the community.
BP 128–47; TTP.

Dissensus (*Le Dissensus*)
A dissensus is not a quarrel over personal interests or opinions. It is a political process that resists juridical litigation and creates a fissure in the sensible order by confronting the established framework of perception, thought, and action with the 'inadmissible', i.e. a **political subject**.
BP 128–47; DW 123–6; TTP.

Distribution of the Sensible (*Le Partage du sensible*)
Occasionally translated as the 'partition of the sensible', *le partage du sensible* refers to the implicit law governing the sensible order that parcels out places and forms of participation in a common world by first establishing the modes of perception within which these are inscribed. The distribution of the sensible thus produces a system of self-evident facts of perception based on the set horizons and modalities of what is visible and audible as well as what can be said, thought, made, or done. Strictly speaking, 'distribution' therefore refers both to forms of inclusion and to forms of exclusion. The 'sensible', of course, does not refer to what shows good sense or judgement but to what is *aisthēton* or capable of being apprehended by the senses.

In the realm of **aesthetics**, Rancière has analysed three different *partages du sensible*: the **ethical regime of images**, the **representative regime of art**, and the **aesthetic regime of art**. In the political domain, he has studied the relationship between the **police**, a totalizing account of the population, and **politics**, the disturbance of the **police** distribution of the sensible by the **subjectivization** of those who have no part in it.
D 57–60, 124–5; HAS; PA 12–13, 42–5; TTP; WA.

Emancipation (*L'Émancipation*)

Neither the teleological end of a political project nor a state of social liberation, the process of emancipation consists in the polemical verification of **equality**. Since this verification is necessarily intermittent and precarious, the logic of emancipation is in fact a heterology, i.e. the introduction of a 'proper-improper' that challenges the **police order**. AT; D 82–3; IS 101–39; PIS; SP 45–52.

Equality (*L'Égalité*)

Although it is the only universal axiom of **politics**, equality nonetheless remains undetermined in its content and lacks an *a priori* foundation. It is, strictly speaking, the presupposition discernible in the polemical reconfigurations of the **police distribution of the sensible**. In other words, Rancière's conception of equality must not be confused with the arithmetical distribution of rights and representation. The essence of equality is not to be found in an equitable unification of interests but in the acts of **subjectivization** that undo the supposedly natural order of the sensible. By treating a **wrong**, **political subjects** transform the aesthetic coordinates of the community in order to implement the only universal in **politics**: we are all equal.
BP 141–2; CM 194–5; D 31–5; DME; DW; IS 45–73; LPA; PA 51–8; PIS; SP 31–6, 80–91; TTP.

Ethical Regime of Images (*Le Régime éthique des images*)

Although the ethical regime predates the **representative** and **aesthetic regimes of art**, it has by no means disappeared in modern times. Its paradigmatic formulation was provided by Plato, who established a rigorous distribution of images – not to be confused with 'art' – in relationship to the ethos of the community. By arranging images according to their origin (the model copied) and their end or purpose (the uses they are put to and the effects they produce), the ethical regime separates artistic simulacra from the true arts, i.e. imitations modelled on the 'truth' whose final aim is to educate the citizenry in accordance with the distribution of occupations in the community.
DI 127–8; PA 20–1, 42–3; PhP; PM 81–5.

Literarity (*La Littérarité*)

Literarity is not a term used to qualify the eternal essence of **literature** or a purely subjective category that is arbitrarily applied to various works of art based on individual sensibilities. It is a unique logic of the sensible, which might be referred to as the democratic regime of the 'orphan letter', where **writing** freely circulates without a legitimating system and thereby undermines the sensible coordinates of the **representative regime of art**. Literarity is thus at one and the same time **literature's** condition of possibility and the paradoxical limit at which literature as such is no longer discernible from any other form of discourse.

CM 115–36; DW 115; LPA; NH 52; PA 39–40; PM 5–14, 81–9, 96.

Literature (*La Littérature*)

As a specific form of artistic production distinct from *les belles-lettres*, literature emerged around the beginning of the nineteenth century and was coextensive with the **aesthetic revolution** that brought into existence the **aesthetic regime of art**. However, literature is much more than a simple mode of artistic production; it is a system of possibilities that abandons the framework of recognition and assessment as well as the codes and hierarchies of the **representative regime of art**. By positing the indifference of form with regard to content and replacing the mimetic principle of fiction with the expressive power of language, literature rejects the poetics of *mimēsis* at the expense of entering into its own interminable contradiction between two forms of **writing**: the 'orphan letter' of democratic **literarity** and the glorious incarnation of truth in the word made flesh.

BP 128–47; CM 14, 114–36, 179–203; LPA; M 103–8; NH 42–60, 99–103; PA 32–4, 36–40, 56–9; PM 5–14, 89, 141–54, 166–76.

Meta-Politics (*La Méta-politique*)

Meta-politics, one of the three principal forms of **political philosophy**, emerges out of Marx's critique of the distance separating the dubious pretences of rights and representation from the hard truth of social reality. It thereby oscillates between two extremes: the condemnation of the ideological illusions of **para-politics** and the appeal to a

communal incarnation of social truth that is strictly homologous with **archi-politics**.
BP 90–1; D 61–93; DW 117–20; LA; PhP.

Ochlos (*L'Okhlos*)
Rancière uses this Greek term meaning 'a throng of people' or 'the multitude' to refer to a community obsessed with its own unification, at the expense of excluding the *dēmos*.
SP 31–6.

Para-Politics (*La Para-politique*)
One of the three kinds of **political philosophy**, para-politics is the result of Aristotle's attempt to square the circle by integrating the egalitarian anarchy of the **dēmos** into the constitutional order of the **police**. This mimetic transformation of the **dēmos** into one of the parties of political litigation, as natural as it may seem to modern theories of sovereignty and the para-political tradition of social contract theory, masks the fact that the **equality** of the *dēmos* can never be adequately accounted for within the **police order**.
D 61–93; DW; PhP.

Partition of the Sensible (*Le Partage du sensible*)
see **Distribution of the Sensible**

People (*Le Peuple*)
This term is not used as a social, economic, political, or ontological category referring to an identifiable group or a pre-constituted collectivity. The 'people' are the **political subjects** of **democracy** that supplement the **police** account of the population and displace the established categories of identification. They are the unaccounted for within the **police order**, the **political subjects** that disclose a **wrong** and demand a redistribution of the sensible order.
CM 126–7; D 22–3, 61–2; PIS; SP 31–6; TTP.

Poetics of Knowledge (*La Poétique du savoir*)
The study of the literary procedures by which a particular form of knowledge establishes itself as a scientific discourse (as was the case,

in the nineteenth century, with sociology, history, and political science).
DW 115–16; NH 8–9, 23, 98–9.

Police or Police Order (*La Police* or *L'Ordre policier*)

As the general law that determines the distribution of parts and roles in a community as well as its forms of exclusion, the **police** is first and foremost an organization of 'bodies' based on a communal **distribution of the sensible**, i.e. a system of coordinates defining modes of being, doing, making, and communicating that establishes the borders between the visible and the invisible, the audible and the inaudible, the sayable and the unsayable. This term should not be confused with *la basse police* or the low-level police force that the word commonly refers to in both French and English. *La basse police* is only one particular instantiation of an overall **distribution of the sensible** that purports to provide a totalizing account of the population by assigning everyone a title and a role within the social edifice. The essence of the police, therefore, is not repression but rather a certain **distribution of the sensible** that precludes the emergence of **politics**. This being the case, there are nonetheless better and worse forms of police, depending on the extent to which the established order remains open to breaches in its 'natural' logic.
BP 7–15; CO; D 21–42, 61–5; DW; ML 40–1; PIS; S 40–1; TTP.

The Political (*Le Politique*)

Although Rancière does not maintain a strict terminological distinction between **politics** (*la politique*) and the political (*le politique*), he often distinguishes the latter as the meeting ground between **politics** and the **police**. In this sense, the political is the terrain upon which the verification of **equality** confronts the established order of identification and classification.
BP 7–15; PIS.

Political Dispute (*Le Litige politique*)
see **Dispute**

Political Philosophy (*La Philosophie politique*)

Rancière has outlined three forms of political philosophy that establish a proper mode of political activity and thereby dissolve, in various

ways, the conflict between **politics** and the **police: archi-politics**, **para-politics**, and **meta-politics**.
D vii–xiii, 61–93; DW 117–20; TTP.

Political Subject (*Le Sujet politique*)

A political subject is neither a political lobby nor an individual who seeks adequate representation for his or her interests and ideas. It is an empty operator that produces cases of political **dispute** by challenging the established framework of identification and classification. Through the process of **subjectivization**, political subjects bring **politics** proper into existence and confront the **police order** with the heterology of **emancipation**. However, the manifestation of politics only occurs via specific acts of implementation, and political subjects forever remain precarious figures that hesitate at the borders of silence maintained by the **police**.
D 35–42, 58–9, 126–7; DME 31–3; DW 115–16; NH 88–95 (democratic subject); PIS; TTP.

Politics (*La Politique*)

If politics has no proper place or predefined subjects for Rancière, this does not mean that everything is political. In its strict sense, politics only exists in intermittent acts of implementation that lack any overall principle or law, and whose only common characteristic is an empty operator: **dissensus**. The essence of politics thus resides in acts of **subjectivization** that separate society from itself by challenging the 'natural order of bodies' in the name of **equality** and polemically reconfiguring the **distribution of the sensible**. Politics is an anarchical process of **emancipation** that opposes the logic of **disagreement** to the logic of the **police**.
BP 7–15; D vii–xiii, 21–42, 61–5, 123; DME; DW; PaA; PIS; S 40–1; TTP.

Post-Democracy (*La Post-démocratie*)

The paradoxical identification of **democracy** with a consensual practice that suppresses political **subjectivization**.
D 95–140; SP 31–6.

Regimes of Art (*Les Régimes de l'art*)

In broad terms, a regime of art is a mode of articulation between three things: ways of doing and making, their corresponding forms of visibility, and ways of conceptualizing both the former and the latter. Rancière has provided detailed accounts of the **ethical regime of images**, the **representative regime of art**, and the **aesthetic regime of art**. In his most recent work, he has introduced the term *régime d'imagéité* ('image regime' or 'imaging regime') to refer to the specific mode of articulation between the visible and the sayable within a given regime of art.

DI 9–39; WA 16–17.

Representative Regime of Art (*Le Régime représentatif de l'art*)

Also referred to as the 'poetic regime of art', the representative regime emerged out of Aristotle's critique of Plato and established a series of axioms that were eventually codified in the Classical Age. The representative regime liberated the arts from the moral, religious, and social criteria of the **ethical regime of images** and separated the fine arts, qua imitations, from other techniques and modes of production. By defining the essence of *poiēsis* as the fictional imitation of actions and isolating a specific domain for fiction, the representative regime did not, however, establish a simple regime of resemblance. Rather than reproducing reality, works within the representative regime obey a series of axioms that define the arts' proper forms: the hierarchy of genres and subject matter, the principle of appropriateness that adapts forms of expression and action to the subjects represented and to the proper genre, the ideal of speech as act that privileges language over the visible imagery that supplements it.

CM 180–1; DI 20–1, 56, 85–8, 120, 125–53; FC 14–18; HAS; IE 21–5, 49–50; LPA; PA 21–2, 35–6, 43; PM 17–30, 43–52; WA.

Sensible, The (*Le Sensible*)
see **Distribution of the Sensible**

Silent Speech (*La Parole muette*)

As one of the central features of the **aesthetic regime of art**, silent speech is the contradictory conjunction between two elements of

this regime. On the one hand, meaning is taken to be immanent in things themselves and, thus, everything – from a building's façade to a woman's face – takes on a voice of its own. On the other hand, however, the mute things of the world only begin to speak if someone deciphers their latent meaning and speaks for them (otherwise they remain completely silent). This contradiction has given birth to at least two major forms of silent speech: the latent meaning beneath the hieroglyphic surface of written signs and the brute presence or *punctum* that remains a deaf and silent obstacle to all forms of signification.
DI 21–2; IE 42; PM.

Subject
see **Political Subject**

Subjectivization (*La Subjectivation*)
Alternately translated as 'subjectification' or 'subjectivation', *la subjectivation* is the process by which a **political subject** extracts itself from the dominant categories of identification and classification. By treating a **wrong** and attempting to implement **equality**, political subjectivization creates a common locus of dispute over those who have no part in the established order. However, the very act of identifying these **political subjects** necessarily has recourse to misnomers, i.e. names that inadequately refer to the anonymous multitude that has no title in the **police order**. The logic of subjectivization is therefore based on the impossible identification of **political subjects**, that is to say subjects who remain unidentifiable in the given field of experience and necessitate 'inaudible' modes of enunciation such as: 'We are all German Jews!'.
D 35–42, 58–9, 126–7; DME 31–3; DW 115–16; PIS; TTP.

Writing (*L'Écriture*)
Writing is not simply a sequence of typographic signs whose printed form is distinct from oral communication. It is a specific **distribution of the sensible** that replaces the **representative regime's** ideal of living speech with a paradoxical form of expression that undermines the legitimate order of discourse. In one respect, writing is the **silent speech** of democratic **literarity** whose 'orphan letter' freely circulates

and speaks to anyone and everyone precisely because it has no living *logos* to direct it. At the same time, however, writing lends itself to the attempt to establish an 'embodied discourse' as the incarnation of the truth of a community. Writing is consequently caught in a continual conflict between democratic **literarity** and the desire to establish a true writing of the word made flesh.
CM 115–36; IE 33–42; NH 56–60; PA 52–60; PaA 203–5; PM 14, 71–2, 81–100.

Wrong (*Le Tort*)

A wrong is a specific form of **equality** that establishes the 'only universal' of **politics** as a polemical point of struggle by relating the manifestation of **political subjects** to the **police order**. Unlike juridical litigation, a wrong does not, therefore, occur between determined parties and cannot be resolved by juridical procedures. A wrong can only be treated by modes of political **subjectivization** that reconfigure the field of experience.
D 3–6, 13, 21–42, 61–3, 78–80, 138–9; PIS.

Appendix II

Bibliography of Primary and Secondary Sources[30]

Books

La Leçon d'Althusser. Paris: Éditions Gallimard, 1974. An English translation of the original critical essay, 'Pour mémoire: sur la théorie de l'idéologie (1969)', appeared as 'On the theory of ideology (the politics of Althusser)', along with a translation of the 'Afterword' from February 1973, in *Radical Philosophy* 7 (Spring 1974): 2–15. 'On the theory of ideology' was reprinted in two works: *Radical Philosophy Reader.* Eds Roy Edgley and Richard Osborne. London: Verso, 1985. 101–36; *Ideology.* Ed. Terry Eagleton. London: Longman Group UK Ltd, 1994. 141–61.

La Nuit des prolétaires: Archives du rêve ouvrier. Paris: Librairie Arthème Fayard, 1981. *The Nights of Labor: The Workers' Dream in Nineteenth-Century France.* John Drury, trans. Introduction by Donald Reid. Philadelphia: Temple University Press, 1989. The introductory chapter to *The Nights of Labor* was previously printed with a 'Preface' by Jonathan Rée as 'Proletarian nights'. Noel Parker, trans. *Radical Philosophy* 31 (Summer 1982): 10–13.

Le Philosophe et ses pauvres. Paris: Librairie Arthème Fayard, 1983. *The Philosopher and His Poor.* John Drury, Corinne Oster, and Andrew Parker, trans. Introduction by Andrew Parker. Durham, NC: Duke University Press, 2004. The first chapter of this work has been published as 'The order of the city'. John Drury, Corinne Oster, Andrew Parker, trans. *Critical Inquiry* 30:2 (Winter 2004): 267–91.

Le Maître ignorant: Cinq Leçons sur l'émancipation intellectuelle. Paris: Librairie Arthème Fayard, 1987. *The Ignorant Schoolmaster: Five Lessons in Intellectual Emancipation.* Kristin Ross, trans. Introduction by Kristin Ross. Stanford: Stanford University Press, 1991.

Courts Voyages au pays du people. Paris: Éditions du Seuil, 1990. *Short Voyages to the Land of the People*. James B. Swenson, trans. Stanford: Stanford University Press, 2003.

Aux Bords du politique. Paris: Éditions Osiris, 1992. *On the Shores of Politics*. Liz Heron, trans. London: Verso, 1995.

Les Mots de l'histoire: Essai de poétique du savoir. Paris: Éditions du Seuil, 1992 [subsequent editions: *Les Noms de l'histoire*]. *The Names of History: On the Poetics of Knowledge*. Hassan Melehy, trans. Foreword by Hayden White. Minneapolis and London: University of Minnesota Press, 1994.

La Mésentente: Politique et philosophie. Paris: Éditions Galilée, 1995. *Disagreement: Politics and Philosophy*. Julie Rose, trans. Minneapolis and London: University of Minnesota Press, 1999.

Mallarmé: La Politique de la sirène. Paris: Hachette Livre, 1996.

Arrêt sur histoire (with Jean-Louis Comolli). Paris: Éditions du Centre Pompidou, 1997.

Aux Bords du politique. Paris: La Fabrique Éditions, 1998. This revised and expanded edition of the work that had originally been published in 1992 includes a number of additional essays, some of which are available in English: 'Politics, identification, and subjectivization' and 'Discussion'. *October* 61 (Summer 1992): 58–64, 78–82; rpt. in *The Identity in Question*. Ed. John Rajchman. New York and London: Routledge, 1995. 63–72; 'The cause of the other'. David Macey, trans. *Parallax* 4:2 (April 1998): 25–33; 'Ten theses on politics'. Davide Panagia, trans. *Theory and Event* 5:3 (2001). <http://muse.jhu.edu/journals/theory_and_event/toc/archive.html#5.3>

La Chair des mots: Politiques de l'écriture. Paris: Éditions Galilée, 1998. *The Flesh of Words: The Politics of Writing*. Charlotte Mandell, trans. Stanford: Stanford University Press, 2004.

La Parole muette: Essai sur les contradictions de la littérature. Paris: Hachette Littératures, 1998.

Le Partage du sensible: Esthétique et politique. Paris: La Fabrique Éditions, 2000. *The Politics of Aesthetics: The Distribution of the Sensible*. Gabriel Rockhill, trans. Introduction by Gabriel Rockhill. Afterword by Slavoj Žižek. London: Continuum Books, 2004.

La Fable cinématographique. Paris: Éditions du Seuil, 2001. *Film Fables*. Emiliano Battista, trans. Oxford: Berg Publishers, forthcoming.

L'Inconscient esthétique. Paris: Éditions Galilée, 2001.

Le Destin des images. Paris: La Fabrique Éditions, 2003.

Les Scènes du peuple: Les Révoltes logiques, 1975/1985. Paris: Horlieu Éditions, 2003.

Edited Works

La Parole ouvrière, 1830–1851 (with Alain Faure). Paris: Union générale d'éditions, 1976.

Le Philosophe plébéien/Gabriel Gauny. Paris: Maspéro/La Découverte; Saint-Denis: Presses Universitaires de Vincennes, 1983.

La Politique des poètes: Pourquoi des poètes en temps de détresse? Paris: Albin Michel, 1992.

Select Articles and Interviews[31]

'Le concept de critique et la critique de l'économie politique'. *Lire le Capital*. Eds. Louis Althusser et al., Paris: François Maspéro, 1965. 81–199. The concluding sections of this article (pages 171–99) were translated as 'The concept of "critique" and the "critique of political economy" (from the *1844 Manuscripts* to *Capital*)'. Ben Brewster, trans. *Economy and Society* 5:3 (August 1976): 352–76. According to the notes to this translation, 'the first three sections were published in the magazine *Theoretical Practice*, numbers one, two and six'. A translation of the entire article is to be found in *Ideology, Method and Marx: Essays from Economy and Society*. Ed. Ali Rattansi. New York and London: Routledge, 1989. 74–180.

'Mode d'emploi pour une réédition de Lire le Capital'. *Les Temps Modernes* 328 (November 1973): 788–807. Rancière adapted this article for an English version under the title 'How to use *Lire le Capital*'. Tanya Asad, trans. *Economy and Society* 5:3 (August 1976): 377–84; rpt. in *Ideology, Method and Marx*. Ed. Ali Rattansi. New York and London: Routledge, 1989. 181–9.

'Le gai savoir'. *Bertolt Brecht, Cahiers de l'Herne* no. 35/1. Paris: Éditions de L'Herne, 1979. 219–37.

'The myth of the artisan: critical reflections on a category of social history'. David H. Lake, trans. *International Labor and Working Class*

History 24 (Fall 1983): 1–16; rpt. in *Work in France: Representations, Meaning, Organization, and Practice.* Eds. Steven Laurence Kaplan and Cynthia J. Koepp. Ithaca: Cornell Univ. Press, 1986. 317–34.

'La représentation de l'ouvrier ou la classe impossible'. *Le Retrait du politique: travaux du Centre de recherches philosophiques sur le politique.* Paris: Éditions Galilée, 1983. 89–111.

'Réponse à Alain Badiou: l'être et l'événement.' *Cahiers du Collège International de Philosophie* 8 (October 1989): 211–25.

'Discovering new worlds: politics of travel and metaphors of space'. *Travellers' Tales: Narratives of Home and Displacement.* Eds. George Robertson et al. New York and London: Routledge, 1994. 29–37.

'Going to the expo: the worker, his wife and machines' and 'Good times or pleasure at the barricades'. John Moore, trans. *Voices of the People: The Social Life of 'La Sociale' at the End of the Second Empire.* Eds. Adrian Rifkin and Roger Thomas. London: Routledge & Kegan Paul, 1988. 23–44; 45–94.

'After what?'. Christina Davis, trans. *Who Comes After the Subject?* Eds. Eduardo Cadava, Peter Connor, and Jean-Luc Nancy. New York and London: Routledge, 1991. 246–52.

'Overlegitimation'. Kristen Ross, trans. *Social Text* 31/32 (1992): 252–7.

'Post-democracy, politics and philosophy: an interview with Jacques Rancière'. Kate Nash, trans. *Angelaki* 1:3 (1994): 171–8.

'Les mots de l'histoire du cinéma'. Interview with Antoine de Baecque. *Cahiers du cinéma* 496 (1995): 48–54.

'The archaeomodern turn'. *Walter Benjamin and the Demands of History.* Ed. Michael P. Steinberg. Ithaca and London: Cornell University Press, 1996. 24–40.

'Sens et figures de l'histoire'. *Face à l'histoire.* Catalogue de l'exposition du Centre Georges Pompidou. Paris: Flammarion, 1996. 20–7.

'Democracy means equality: Jacques Rancière interviewed by *Passages*'. David Macey, trans. *Radical Philosophy* 82 (March/April 1997): 29–36.

'Existe-t-il une esthétique deleuzienne?'. *Gilles Deleuze: Une Vie philosophique.* Ed. Eric Alliez. Le Plessis-Robinson: Institut Synthélabo, 1998. 525–36. 'Is there a Deleuzian aesthetics?'. Radmila Djordjevic, trans. *Qui Parle*, 14:2 (2004).

'L'historicité du cinéma'. *De L'Histoire au cinéma*. Eds. Antoine de Baecque and Christian Delage. Bruxelles: Éditions Complexe, 1998. 45–60.

'Dissenting words – a conversation with Jacques Rancière'. Interview with Davide Panagia. Davide Panagia, trans. *Diacritics: A Review of Contemporary Criticism* 30:2 (2000): 113–26.

'Interview with Jacques Rancière: cinematographic image, democracy, and the "splendor of the insignificant"'. Interview with Solange Guenoun. Alyson Waters, trans. *Sites: The Journal of 20th-Century Contemporary French Studies* 4 (2000): 249–58.

'Jacques Rancière: history and the art system'. Interview with Yan Ciret. *Art Press* 258 (June 2000): 18–23.

'Jacques Rancière: literature, politics, aesthetics: approaches to democratic disagreement'. Interview with Solange Guenoun and James H. Kavanagh. Roxanne Lapidus, trans. *SubStance: A Review of Theory and Literary Criticism* 29 (2000): 3–24.

'What aesthetics can mean'. *From an Aesthetic Point of View: Philosophy, Art and the Senses*. Ed. Peter Osborne. London: The Serpent's Tail, 2000. 13–33.

'Le 11 septembre et après: une rupture de l'ordre symbolique?'. *Lignes* 8 (May, 2002): 35–46.

'The aesthetic revolution and its outcomes'. *New Left Review* 14 (March/April 2002): 133–51.

'La communauté esthétique'. *Politique de la parole: Singularité et communauté*. Ed. Pierre Ouellet. Montréal: Éditions Trait d'union, 2002. 145–66.

'Esthétique, inesthétique, anti-esthétique'. *Alain Badiou: Penser le multiple*. Ed. Charles Ramond. Paris: L'Harmattan, 2002. 477–96. 'Aesthetics, inaesthetics, anti-aesthetics'. Ray Brassier, trans. *Think Again: Alain Badiou and the Future of Philosophy*. Ed. Peter Hallward. London: Continuum, 2004. 218–31.

'Metamorphosis of the muses'. *Sonic Process*. Actar Editorial, 2003. 17–30.

'Politics and aesthetics: an interview'. Interview with Peter Hallward. Forbes Morlock, trans. *Angelaki* 8:2 (August 2003): 191–211.

'The thinking of dissensus: politics and aesthetics'. *Fidelity to the Disagreement: Jacques Rancière and the Political* (conference organized by the Post-Structuralism and Radical Politics specialist group). London: Goldsmiths College, 16–17 September, 2003. <http://homepages.gold.ac.uk/psrpsg/ranciere.doc>

'Godard, Hitchcock and the cinematographic image'. *For Ever Godard.* Eds. Michael Temple, James Williams, and Michael Witt. London: Black Dog Publishing and Phaidon Press, 2004.

'Who is the subject of the rights of man?'. *South Atlantic Quarterly* 103:2–3 (Spring/Summer 2004).

'From Lyotard to Schiller: two readings of Kant and their political significance'. *Radical Philosophy*, forthcoming.

Further Reading

Badiou, Alain. 'Rancière et la communauté des égaux' and 'Rancière et l'apolitique'. *Abrégé de métapolitique.* Paris: Éditions du Seuil, 1998. 121–38.

Benton, Ted. 'Discussion: Rancière on ideology'. *Radical Philosophy* 9 (Winter 1974): 27–8.

Craib, Ian. 'Rancière and Althusser'. *Radical Philosophy* 10 (Spring 1975): 28–9.

Deranty, Jean-Philippe. 'Jacques Rancière's contribution to the ethics of recognition'. *Political Theory* 31:1 (February 2003): 136–56.

During, Elie. 'What pure aesthetics can't do'. *Art Press* 267 (April 2001): 56–8.

Engelibert, Jean-Paul. 'Sur Jacques Rancière'. *Literary Research/ Recherche littéraire* 30 (Fall–Winter 1998): 23–32.

Gibson, Andrew. 'Rancière and the "limit" of realism'. *Realism and Its Discontents.* Eds. Danuta Fjellestad and Elizabeth Kella. Karlskrona, Sweden: Blekinge Institute of Technology, 2003. 56–69.

Gibson, Andrew. '"And the wind wheezing through that organ once in a while": voice, narrative, film'. *New Literary History* 32:3 (Summer 2001): 639–57.

Hirst, Paul. 'Rancière, ideology, and capital'. *On Law and Ideology.* London and Basingstoke: The Macmillan Press LTD, 1979. 75–95.

Labelle, Gilles. 'Two refoundation projects of democracy in contemporary French philosophy: Cornelius Castoriadis and Jacques Rancière'. Nancy Renault, trans. *Philosophy and Social Criticism* 27:4 (July, 2001): 75–103.

Mehlman, Jeffrey. 'Teaching reading: the case of Marx in France'. *Diacritics: A Review of Contemporary Criticism* 6:4 (Winter 1976): 10–18.

Panagia, Davide. '*Ceci n'est pas un argument*: an introduction to the ten theses'. *Theory and Event* 5:3 (2001). <http://muse.jhu.edu/journals/theory_and_event/toc/archive.html#5.3>

Ross, Kristin. *May '68 and Its Afterlives*. Chicago: University of Chicago Press, 2003.

Ross, Kristin. 'Rancière and the practice of equality'. *Social Text* 29 (1991): 57–71.

Valentine, Jeremy. 'The hegemony of hegemony'. *History of the Human Sciences* 14:1 (February 2001): 88–104.

Watts, Philip. 'Le cinéma entre *mimésis* et zone d'ombre'. *Critique* 58:665 (October, 2002): 830–7.

Žižek, Slavoj. 'Political subjectivization and its vicissitudes'. *The Ticklish Subject*. London: Verso, 1999. 171–244.

Special Issues on Rancière

Critique 53:601–602 (June–July 1997). Contents: Philippe Roger, 'Présentation'; Yves Michaud, 'Les pauvres et leur philosophe: la philosophie de Jacques Rancière'; Patrick Cingolani, 'Modernité, démocratie, hérésie'; Arlette Farge, 'L'histoire comme avènement'; Pierre Campion, 'Mallarmé à la lumière de la raison poétique'; Jacques Rancière, 'La parole muette: notes sur "la littérature"'.

Theory and Event 6:4 (2003) Contents: Jean-Philippe Deranty, 'Rancière and contemporary political ontology'; Davide Panagia, 'Thinking with and against the "ten theses"'; Michael Dillon, '(De)void of politics?: a response to Jacques Rancière's "ten theses on politics"'; Aamir R. Mufti, 'Reading Jacques Rancière's "ten theses on politics": after September 11th'; Kirstie M. McClure, 'Disconnections, connections, and questions: reflections of Jacques Rancière's "ten theses on politics"'; Jacques Rancière, 'Comments and responses'. <http://muse.jhu.edu/journals/theory_and_event/toc/archive.html#6.4>

SubStance: A Review of Theory and Literary Criticism 103, 33:1 (2004). Contents: Eric Méchoulan, 'Introduction'; Jacques Rancière, 'The politics of literature'; Solange Guénoun, 'Jacques Rancière's Freudian cause'; Gabriel Rockhill, 'The silent revolution'; Jean-

Louis Déotte, 'The differences between Rancière's *Mésentente* (political disagreement) and Lyotard's *Différend*'; Tom Conley, 'A fable of film: Rancière's Anthony Mann'; Michèle Garneau, 'Film's aesthetic turn: a contribution from Jacques Rancière'; David F. Bell, 'Writing, movement/space, democracy: on Jacques Rancière's literary history'.

Notes

1   Without excessively multiplying the examples, it is worth highlighting the unique logic of translation operative in the work of the French *belles infidèles* in the seventeenth century. They brazenly adapted *les Anciens* to the poetic norms of *les Modernes* and often changed what were seen to be the inadequacies of the original work (including anything from vocabulary and stylistics to plot structure and organization, which sometimes necessitated significant omissions). It is a grave but nonetheless common mistake to impose a teleological model on the history of translation, denigrating the *belles infidèles* and extolling the scientific superiority of contemporary translation practice, which began approximately with the Romantics. The logic of signification at work in specific historical communities cannot be readily translated into one single overarching logic of meaning that would define the trans-historical nature of translation. For more on the history of translation, see the work of Antoine Berman, Henri Meschonnic, George Steiner, and Henri Van Hoof.

2   I am not arguing in favour of what Schleiermacher referred to as a method of translation that brings the author toward the reader. I am pragmatically advocating the use of a relational logic of signification in a specific socio-historic situation and with a particular type of disourse.

3   An earlier, abbreviated version of this essay appeared in the *Encyclopedia of Modern French Thought* (New York and London: Fitzroy Dearborn, 2004).

4   The numbers in square brackets refer to the pagination of the original French edition (Paris : La Fabrique – Éditions, 2000) and correspond to the beginning of each page indicated. – Trans.

5   *Le commun* – alternately translated as 'something in common', 'something common', 'what is common', or 'what is common to the community' – is strictly speaking what makes or produces

a community and not simply an attribute shared by all of its members. The adjectival form of the same word, *commun*, is translated as 'common', 'shared', or 'communal' depending on the context. – Trans.

6   Rancière uses the word 'poem' (*le poème*) in reference to the Greek term *poiēma*, which means 'anything made or done' as well as 'a piece of craftsmanship', 'a poetic work', or 'an act or deed'. He also sometimes prefers 'the stage' (*la scène*) over 'theatre' or 'drama' (*le théâtre*), undoubtedly in order to emphasize the public aspect of theatrical performances on the *skēnē*. – Trans.

7   From this perspective, it is possible to understand the paralogism inherent in all of the attempts to deduce the characteristics of the arts from the ontological status of images (for example, the incessant attempts to derive the idea of the 'distinctive feature' of painting, photography, or film from the theology of the icon). This attempt establishes a relationship of cause and effect between properties of two regimes of thought that are mutually exclusive. The same problem is raised by Benjamin's analysis of the aura insofar as he establishes a questionable deduction from the ritual value of the image to the value of the unicity of the work of art: 'It is a fact of decisive importance that the existence of the work of art with reference to its aura is never entirely separated from its ritual function. In other words, the unique value of the "authentic" work of art has its basis in ritual, the location of its original use value' ('The work of art in the age of mechanical reproduction'. *Illuminations*. Ed. Hannah Arendt. Harry Zohn, trans. New York: Harcourt, Brace & World, 1968, p. 225 [translation slightly modified in order to maintain an overall coherence between the quotation and Rancière's commentary – Trans.]). This 'fact' is in reality only the problematic adaptation between two schemata of transformation: the historicizing schema of the 'secularization of the sacred' and the economic schema of the transformation of use value into exchange value. However, when sacred service defines the purpose of the statue or painting as images, the very idea of a specificity of art and of a property of unicity inherent in its 'works' cannot come to light. The erasure of the former is necessary for the emergence of the latter. It by no means follows that the idea

of art's specificity is an altered form of the definition of images by sacred service. The 'in other words' assumes two propositions to be equivalent that are not in the least and allows for all of the crossing-over between the materialist explanation of art and its transformation into secular theology. This is how Benjamin's theorization of the transition from cult value to exhibition value today supports three competing discourses: the discourse that celebrates the modern demystification of artistic mysticism, the discourse that endows the work of art and its exhibition-space with the sacred values of the representation of the invisible, and the discourse that contrasts the buried ages when the gods were still present with the age of abandonment, the age of man's 'being-exposed'.

8   Cf. Raymond Bellour. 'La chambre'. *L'Entre-images 2*. Paris: P.O.L., 1999. 281–317.

9   'Subjective' here refers to the political process of 'subjectivization' as it is explained in Appendix 1. – Trans.

10 'L'inoubliable'. Jean-Louis Comolli and Jacques Rancière. *Arrêt sur histoire*. Paris: Centre Georges-Pompidou, 1997. 47–70.

11 The anti-modernist, polemical vocation of this late discovery of the 'origin' of photography, modelled on the myth of the invention of painting by Dibutades, clearly appears in the work of Roland Barthes (*Camera Lucida*) as well as in the work of Rosalind Krauss (*Le Photographique*).

12 Rancière uses 'the commonplace' (*le quelconque*) to refer to both the ordinary and everyday as well as to the insignificant, i.e. the mass of anonymous objects or people that lack any specific quality or value. – Trans.

13 Here as elsewhere, Rancière uses the word 'body' (*le corps*) in the largest possible sense of the term in order to refer alternately – and sometimes simultaneously – to physical forms (anything from the bodies of human beings to objects or buildings), communities (social bodies), political configurations (the body politic), units of discourse (bodies of writing), and even geographic formations (bodies of land and water). – Trans.

14 The French term *histoire* means both 'history' and 'story'. Although the context often provides clear indications for deciding between

these two alternatives, Rancière occasionally plays off of the ambiguity in French (rendered in English as 'history or story'). – Trans.

15   Jacques Rancière. 'La fiction de mémoire: à propos du *Tombeau d'Alexandre* de Chris Marker'. *Trafic* 29 (Spring 1999): 36–47. [A revised version of this article was later published as a chapter in *La Fable cinématographique* (Paris: Éditions du Seuil, 2001. 201–16). An English translation of this work is forthcoming. – Trans.]

16   On Rancière's use of the word 'poem', see note 6. Rancière uses the term 'poetry' (*la poésie*) in the following pages to refer to the Greek term *poiēsis*, which means 'the art of poetry' or 'a poem' as well as 'a making, a forming, a creating'. – Trans.

17   Balzac's *La Peau de chagrin* has also been translated into English as *The Wild Ass's Skin*. – Trans.

18   On Rancière's use of the term 'body', see note 13. – Trans.

19   Regarding this issue, I take the liberty of referring the reader to my book, *The Names of History: On the Poetics of Knowledge* (Hassan Melehy, trans. Minneapolis: The University of Minnesota Press, 1994).

20   Rancière is concerned with the relationship between *l'art* et *le travail* in this chapter. The general term 'work' was appropriate in most cases as a translation of *le travail*. However, certain contexts and expressions required using 'labour' to translate the same term in French. – Trans.

21   On Rancière's notion of *le commun*, see note 5. – Trans.

22   This interview was originally conducted in French on October 18th, 2003 and was later reviewed by Jacques Rancière. – Trans.

23   *The Names of History: On the Poetics of Knowledge*. Hassan Melehy, trans. Minneapolis and London: University of Minnesota Press, 1994, p. 52 (*Les Mots de l'histoire*. Paris: Éditions du Seuil, 1992, p. 109). Translation slightly modified. – Trans.

24   On Rancière's use of the word 'poetry', see note 16. – Trans.

25   Rimbaud's '*Alchimie du verbe*' contains an implicit reference to Lemaître de Sacy's translation of the Gospel according to St. John: '*Au commencement était le Verbe*'. The King James version and other major English translations prefer to render *logos* as

'Word' ('In the beginning was the Word'), thereby leading to the English translation of Rimbaud's poem as 'The Alchemy of the Word'. For this reason, the term 'word' has been used here as a translation of '*verbe*'.

26 Rancière frequently adopts the standard vocabulary of other writers in order to implicitly reference their work instead of making explicit references or using quotations. This type of lexical appropriation can often be transferred directly into English due to a similar network of intellectual or cultural connotations (for instance, *spectacle* and spectacle both evoke, in certain contexts, the work of Guy Debord). However, whereas *désœuvrement* immediately conjures up the work of Maurice Blanchot in French, Ann Smock's standard translation of this term as 'inertia' does not have the same effect in English. Hence the decision to supplement it with the term 'non-work' and add the present commentary. – Trans.

27 Whereas the 'plastic arts' (sculpture, ceramics, etc.) are often opposed to the art of drawing and painting in English, *les arts plastiques* include any of the arts that elaborate concrete aesthetic forms (sculpture, ceramics, architecture, drawing, painting, etc.). The use of the term 'plastic', both here and elsewhere, refers to this larger semantic field. – Trans.

28 'A child kills himself'. *Short Voyages to the Land of the People*. James B. Swenson, trans. Stanford: Stanford University Press, 2003. 107–34. *Europa '51* was released in 1952 in the United Kingdom as *No Greater Love* and in 1954 in the United States as *The Greatest Love*. – Trans.

29 To avoid any confusion, it is worth noting that the French tradition tends to translate John 3:8 ('*to pneuma hopou thelei pneî*') as '*l'Esprit souffle où il veut*', whereas the English translators generally prefer something closer to 'the wind blows where it wills'. *Pneuma* refers equally to the wind and to spirit. – Trans.

30 Some of the information compiled in this bibliography is dependent on databases and existing bibliographies that, on more than one occasion, proved to be less reliable than one would hope. For this reason, a concerted effort was made to directly consult all of the works cited in order to correct any errors. Nevertheless,

Index

The page numbers in bold refer to entries in the 'Glossary of Technical Terms'.